The Awful Speller's Dictionary

Edited and compiled by
Joseph Krevisky
and
Jordan L. Linfield
British Edition Revised
by

GUINNESS PUBLISHING

First published in the USA by
Innovation Press, New York, under the title
A Handbook for Terrible Spellers: The Backwords Dictionary

Published 1991 in Great Britain by
Guinness Publishing Ltd,
33 London Road, Enfield, Middlesex

Typeset in Century Schoolbook by
Ace Filmsetting Ltd, Frome, Somerset
Printed and bound in Great Britain by
BPCC Hazell Books
Aylesbury, Bucks, England
Member of BPCC Ltd.

A catalogue record for this book is available from the British Library.

ISBN 0-85112-986-2

INTRODUCTION

All of us have trouble, at one time or another, with our spelling. This book is designed for those of you who are bright, educated, and hold responsible positions, but who are - let's face it - awful spellers. If you are a secretary, you know how often your boss makes a mistake in spelling; if you are a student, you know that even your teacher or professor misspells. Doctors, lawyers, professional footballers, even Members of Parliament are known to misspell. Why?

IT'S OUR ENGLISH LANGUAGE

If you're unsure of your spelling, it is by no means your fault. It's due to the fact that very often there is no rhyme or reason for the spelling of a great many words in the English language.

As an example, take the sound of the letter **f**. It can be spelt **gh**, **ph**, **ft**, as well as **f**. The following words illustrate the above variations.

enou**gh** **ph**one o**ft**en **f**un

None other than George Bernard Shaw created the following spellings, just to point out the inconsistencies in our language:

fish - GHOTI
potato - GHOUGHPTEIGHBTEAU

Stumped? Here's the solution:

FISH

gh as in enough **o** as in women **ti** as in nation

Sure enough, it's FISH!

POTATO is even more fun:

p as in hiccough
o as in though
t as in ptomaine
a as in neigh
t as in debt
o as in bureau

HOW TO USE THE AWFUL SPELLER'S DICTIONARY

Dictionaries, as you know, are wonderful tools for everyone who reads and writes. There is just one catch: you must know who to spell a word correctly in order to find it in an ordinary dictionary.

Not so with *The Awful Speller's Dictionary*. We have arranged thousands of spelling demons according to their common misspellings. No longer do you have to hunt and seek through many pages for a correct spelling. In *The Awful Speller's Dictionary* you simply look up any word as you think it might be spelt – the correct spelling follows. For example:

The **sergeant** and the **colonel** had **ptomaine** poisoning. If you wanted to check the spelling of these three words you could spend hours looking them up in the standard dictionary under the headings of:

sar **ker** **to**

We have eliminated this problem entirely. NOW YOU DO NOT HAVE TO KNOW THE CORRECT SPELLING OF A WORD IN ORDER TO FIND IT. Simply look up the word as you think it is spelt in the left-hand column of incorrect spellings. If you are misspelling, you will find the word in alphabetical sequence in the left-hand column with the correct spelling in the right-hand column.

If you do not find it in the incorrect spelling list, you are most likely spelling correctly. To make sure, check your spellings in the **QUICK LIST OF CORRECT SPELLINGS** in the back of the book. Here, all the spelling demons are arranged alphabetically by their correct spellings.

Take the word **sergeant**. Suppose you thought it was spelt **sargent**. Look up the word your way:

Incorrect	**Correct**
sargent	**sergeant**

Or suppose you were in doubt as to the spelling of the word **ptomaine.** You're not sure if the word begins with a **p** or a **t**. You lean towards the **t**, however, and following your inclination you will find:

Incorrect	**Correct**
tomaine	**ptomaine**

If you had looked for **ptomaine** under **p** you would not have found it because you were spelling it correctly. Just double check in the short alphabetical **QUICK LIST OF CORRECT SPELLINGS** at the end of the book.

LOOK-ALIKES OR SOUND-ALIKES

Very often, spelling mistakes are made because we confuse words which look alike or sound alike. For example, **to, too**, and **two**; or **it's** and **its**. We have arranged hundreds of such troublesome pairs in the **Look-Alikes or Sound-Alikes** sections of this book, which are found at the end of each letter of the alphabet. A brief definition or key identifying word is given, so that you know immediately which word to use and spell correctly.

SOURCES OF THE WORDS

Some of you may be amazed at the extent and types of spelling errors found in *The Awful Speller's Dictionary*. You might even scoff, 'Nobody spells like that!' But those of you have been exposed to correspondence, stories, advertisements, and articles know just how bad the situation is. The misspellings in this book were compiled from real-life examples in students' tests and essays, office correspondence, ads, articles and stories in print and in manuscript, signs, official notices, and in studies of spelling. The headline writer who wrote about teenagers sniffing 'viles' of glue (see our look-alikes and sound-alikes) may be saying more than with correct spelling, but it is still wrong.

It is interesting that there is no single pattern of misspelling. This may be one reason why there is a paucity of literature dealing with the causes of spelling errors. We know that phonetic spelling is a key source, but it is far from the only one. Regional speech dialects, transposition of letters, and illogic, all play their role, but a definitive study on the causes of misspelling is yet to be done.

A WORD OF CAUTION

Keep *The Awful Speller's Dictionary* close at hand. It should be on your desk, at your typewriter, in your briefcase. Refer to it whenever you are in doubt. Try it on your family or friends one night when the TV set is broken.

a

Incorrect	Correct
abbandon	**abandon**
abbolition	**abolition**
abcess	**abscess**
abdeman	**abdomen**
abel	**able**
abillity	**ability**
abiss	**abyss**
abolishion	**abolition**
abreviate	**abbreviate**
abrup	**abrupt**
absalutuly	**absolutely**
abscence	**absence**
absenteism	**absenteeism**
abserd	**absurd**
absess	**abscess**
absint	**absent**
abuze	**abuse**
abzurd	**absurd**
accademic	**academic**
acceed	**accede**
accellarate	**accelerate**
accerasy	**accuracy**
accesible	**accessible**
accidently	**accidentally**
acclame	**acclaim**
accnowledge	**acknowledge**
accomodate	**accommodate**
accoustics	**acoustics**
accownt	**account**
accrew	**accrue**
accrobat	**acrobat**
accross	**across**
accrostic	**acrostic**
accseed	**accede**
accumalate	**accumulate**
accumen	**acumen**
accur	**occur**
accurecy	**accuracy**
accurit	**accurate**
accute	**acute**
acend	**ascend**
acer	**acre**
acertain	**ascertain**
acess	**assess**
acheive	**achieve**
ackwire	**acquire**
aclimate	**acclimate**
acnowledgement	**acknowledgement**
acnowledge	**acknowledge**
acommodate	**accommodate**
acompany	**accompany**
acomplice	**accomplice**
acomplish	**accomplish**
acord	**accord**
acording	**according**

Incorrect	Correct
acordion	**accordion**
acost	**accost**
acount	**account**
acountent	**accountant**
acquantence	**acquaintance**
acquasition	**acquisition**
acquitle	**acquittal**
acrabat	**acrobat**
acredit	**accredit**
acrege	**acreage**
acrew	**accrue**
acros	**across**
acrost	**across**
acrue	**accrue**
acsesery	**accessory**
acsess	**access**
acshual	**actual**
acsident	**accident**
acter	**actor**
actualy	**actually**
acuaduct	**aqueduct**
acuire	**acquire**
acumenacal	**ecumenical**
acumulate	**accumulate**
acuse	**accuse**
acustom	**accustom**
acuze	**accuse**
acwitt	**acquit**
adaquete	**adequate**
addement	**adamant**
addhere	**adhere**

Incorrect	Correct
addick	**addict**
addministeration	**administration**
addmiral	**admiral**
addmit	**admit**
addorible	**adorable**
addult	**adult**
adelesense	**adolescence**
adequatly	**adequately**
adged	**aged**
adgitator	**agitator**
adict	**addict**
adige	**adage**
adishon	**edition**
adition	**addition**
adjatent	**adjutant**
adjern	**adjourn**
adjustible	**adjustable**
admendment	**amendment**
admerable	**admirable**
administrater	**administrator**
admissable	**admissible**
admitance	**admittance**
admition	**admission**
adolesent	**adolescent**
adop	**adopt**
adress	**address**
advanse	**advance**
advantagous	**advantageous**
advantige	**advantage**

Incorrect	Correct
advertisment	**advertisement**
advisery	**advisory**
advisor	**adviser**
advizable	**advisable**
advizer	**adviser**
aeriel	**aerial**
afair	**affair**
afect	**affect**
affraid	**afraid**
Affrica	**Africa**
Afgan	**Afghan**
afible	**affable**
afidavit	**affidavit**
afiliate	**affiliate**
afirm	**affirm**
afix	**affix**
aflict	**afflict**
afluence	**affluence**
aford	**afford**
aforizm	**aphorism**
afrade	**afraid**
Africer	**Africa**
afront	**affront**
afterwerds	**afterwards**
agast	**aghast**
agencys	**agencies**
agenst	**against**
agensy	**agency**
agern	**adjourn**
agervate	**aggravate**
aggragate	**aggregate**
aggrarian	**agrarian**
aggree	**agree**
aggresive	**aggressive**
aggriculture	**agriculture**
agground	**aground**
aging	**ageing**
aginst	**against**
agrandize	**aggrandize**
agravate	**aggravate**
agreable	**agreeable**
agregate	**aggregate**
agreing	**agreeing**
agressive	**aggressive**
agricultral	**agricultural**
ahmond	**almond**
aile	**aisle**
airea	**area**
aireel	**aerial**
airis	**heiress**
airoplane	**aeroplane**
aithe	**eighth**
ajacent	**adjacent**
ajenda	**agenda**
ajoining	**adjoining**
ajurn	**adjourn**
ajustable	**adjustable**
ajutent	**adjutant**
ake	**ache**
aker	**acre**
aklaim	**acclaim**
akne	**acne**
akseed	**accede**

Incorrect	Correct
aksent	**accent**
akses	**axis**
aksess	**access**
akward	**awkward**
aleby	**alibi**
aleet	**élite**
alege	**allege**
alegiance	**allegiance**
alergy	**allergy**
aleveate	**alleviate**
alfabet	**alphabet**
alian	**alien**
aliance	**alliance**
aline	**align**
alkohol	**alcohol**
alledge	**allege**
allee	**alley**
allegy	**allergy**
allert	**alert**
allie	**ally**
allmanac	**almanac**
allmighty	**almighty**
allmost	**almost**
allone	**alone**
alloting	**allotting**
allottment	**allotment**
allowence	**allowance**
allready	**already**
allso	**also**
allthough	**although**
alltogether	**altogether**
alluminum	**aluminium**

Incorrect	Correct
allways	**always**
alocate	**allocate**
alot	**allot**
aloted	**allotted**
alow	**allow**
alowed	**allowed**
alright	**all right**
altenate	**alternate**
altrueizm	**altruism**
amada	**armada**
amature	**amateur**
ambbasador	**ambassador**
ambbiguous	**ambiguous**
ambidextarous	**ambidextrous**
ambulence	**ambulance**
amealiorate	**ameliorate**
amerous	**amorous**
amissable	**admissible**
ammend	**amend**
Ammerican	**American**
ammonition	**ammunition**
ammonya	**ammonia**
ammount	**amount**
amond	**almond**
amonia	**ammonia**
amoor	**amour**
amoung	**among**
amunition	**ammunition**
amusment	**amusement**
aminable	**amenable**
ammiable	**amiable**

Incorrect	Correct
ammity	**amity**
amyable	**amiable**
analasis	**analysis**
analise	**analyse**
anartic	**antarctic**
anaversary	**anniversary**
anceint	**ancient**
ancle	**ankle**
anex	**annex**
angziety	**anxiety**
anihilate	**annihilate**
aniversery	**anniversary**
ankel	**ankle**
anker	**anchor**
ankshus	**anxious**
annalasis	**analysis**
annalog	**analogue**
annalogy	**analogy**
annecdote	**anecdote**
annew	**anew**
annoint	**anoint**
annonymous	**anonymous**
anntena	**antenna**
annuel	**annual**
annull	**annul**
anonimus	**anonymous**
anotate	**annotate**
anouncement	**announcement**
anoyence	**annoyance**
anser	**answer**
ansester	**ancestor**

Incorrect	Correct
ansestree	**ancestry**
anshent	**ancient**
antartic	**antarctic**
antchovy	**anchovy**
antebiotic	**antibiotic**
ante-British	**anti-British**
anteceptic	**antiseptic**
antedote	**antidote**
anteek	**antique**
antisapate	**anticipate**
antisedent	**antecedent**
anual	**annual**
anualee	**annually**
anuity	**annuity**
anull	**annul**
anuther	**another**
anwser	**answer**
anytime	**any time**
any where	**anywhere**
aparant	**apparent**
aparatus	**apparatus**
aparel	**apparel**
aparent	**apparent**
apeal	**appeal**
apear	**appear**
apease	**appease**
apeerence	**appearance**
apellate	**appellate**
apendectomy	**appendectomy**
apendix	**appendix**
apetite	**appetite**

Incorrect	Correct
aplaud	**applaud**
apliance	**appliance**
aplicant	**applicant**
aply	**apply**
apoint	**appoint**
apoligize	**apologize**
apologeticly	**apologetically**
apologys	**apologies**
aposle	**apostle**
appaling	**appalling**
appartment	**apartment**
appeel	**appeal**
appellete	**appellate**
appere	**appear**
apperence	**appearance**
apperture	**aperture**
applys	**applies**
appointy	**appointee**
appologize	**apologize**
appology	**apology**
appostrophe	**apostrophe**
appraisel	**appraisal**
aprecot	**apricot**
appreshiate	**appreciate**
appresible	**appreciable**
approch	**approach**
approove	**approve**
appropo	**apropos**
apptitude	**aptitude**
apraise	**appraise**
apreciate	**appreciate**
aprehend	**apprehend**
aprentice	**apprentice**
aprin	**apron**
aproach	**approach**
apropo	**apropos**
apropriate	**appropriate**
aprove	**approve**
aproximate	**approximate**
aquaintance	**acquaintance**
aquiesce	**acquiesce**
aquire	**acquire**
aquisition	**acquisition**
aquittal	**acquittal**
araign	**arraign**
arange	**arrange**
arbatrate	**arbitrate**
arbitery	**arbitrary**
archetect	**architect**
ardvark	**aardvark**
aready	**already**
arears	**arrears**
arest	**arrest**
argueing	**arguing**
arguement	**argument**
arial	**aerial**
ariseing	**arising**
arithmatic	**arithmetic**
arive	**arrive**
arize	**arise**
arkaic	**archaic**
arkitect	**architect**

Incorrect	Correct
arkives	**archives**
armastice	**armistice**
armfull	**armful**
arodynamics	**aerodynamics**
arogant	**arrogant**
Aron	**Aaron**
aronautics	**aeronautics**
arosol	**aerosol**
arouseing	**arousing**
arow	**arrow**
arowse	**arouse**
arragent	**arrogant**
arrangment	**arrangement**
arrise	**arise**
arrivel	**arrival**
arround	**around**
arrouse	**arouse**
artaficial	**artificial**
artic	**arctic**
artical	**article**
artilery	**artillery**
artisticly	**artistically**
artry	**artery**
asanine	**asinine**
asassin	**assassin**
asassinate	**assassinate**
asault	**assault**
ase	**ace**
asemble	**assemble**
asent	**assent**
asert	**assert**

Incorrect	Correct
asess	**assess**
aset	**asset**
asfalt	**asphalt**
ashin	**ashen**
ashure	**assure**
asid	**acid**
asign	**assign**
asist	**assist**
asistent	**assistant**
asma	**asthma**
asociate	**associate**
asort	**assort**
aspirent	**aspirant**
asprin	**aspirin**
assale	**assail**
assesed	**assessed**
assimilateable	**assimilable**
assine	**assign**
assinine	**asinine**
assistence	**assistance**
asswage	**assuage**
assylum	**asylum**
ast	**asked**
astablish	**establish**
asternot	**astronaut**
asume	**assume**
asure	**assure**
asurence	**assurance**
atach	**attach**
atack	**attack**
atact	**attacked**
atain	**attain**

Incorrect	Correct
atempt	**attempt**
atemt	**attempt**
atend	**attend**
atendence	**attendance**
atendent	**attendant**
atenshun	**attention**
atest	**attest**
athalete	**athlete**
athaletic	**athletic**
athority	**authority**
athyist	**atheist**
atic	**attic**
atire	**attire**
atitude	**attitude**
atlete	**athlete**
atmisfere	**atmosphere**
atorney	**attorney**
atract	**attract**
atrosity	**atrocity**
attatude	**attitude**
attemp	**attempt**
auctionier	**auctioneer**
audable	**audible**
audiance	**audience**
Augest	**August**
aukward	**awkward**
autamatic	**automatic**
autamobile	**automobile**
auther	**author**
authodox	**orthodox**
automashun	**automation**
auxilary	**auxiliary**
avalable	**available**
avantage	**advantage**
aveater	**aviator**
aved	**avid**
avilanch	**avalanche**
avocate	**advocate**
avoidible	**avoidable**
avrage	**average**
aw	**awe**
awdiance	**audience**
awditoriem	**auditorium**
awefel	**awful**
awf	**off**
awkwid	**awkward**
aw revoir	**au revoir**
awt	**ought**
awthentick	**authentic**
awthorety	**authority**
awtimaticly	**automatically**
awtum	**autumn**
axes	**axis**
axident	**accident**
aypron	**apron**
aytheist	**atheist**
Azher	**Asia**
azma	**asthma**

Look-Alikes or Sound-Alikes

Abel *name* • **able** *strong*

abjure *renounce* • **adjure** *entreat*

accede *agree* • **exceed** *go beyond*

accept *receive* • **except** *omit*

accent *speech* • **ascent** *rise* • **assent** *agree*

access *admittance* • **excess** *extra*

acentric *not centred* • **eccentric** *strange*

acerb *bitter* • **a Serb** *a Yugoslav*

acts *to perform on stage, things done* • **axe** *a tool*

adapt *make fit* • **adept** *expert* • **adopt** *take in*

addable *can be added* • **edible** *can be eaten*

addition *add* • **edition** *issue*

adds *increases* • **ads** *advertisements* • **adze** *tool*

adieu *farewell* • **ado** *commotion*

adjoin *next to* • **adjourn** *put off*

adjure *entreat* • **abjure** *renounce*

ado *commotion* • **adieu** *farewell*

ads *advertisements* • **adze** *a cutting tool* • **adds** *increaes*

adverse *against* • **averse** *unwilling*

advice *suggestion* • **advise** *to suggest*

adze *a cutting tool* • **ads** *advertisements* • **adds** *increases*

aerie *eagle's nest* • **eerie** *ghostly* • **eery** *eerie*

affect *act or influence* • **effect** *result of action or to bring about*

affective *emotional* • **effective** *impressive, operative*

aid *help* • **aide** *assistant*

aigrette *ornamental plume* • **egret** *heron*

ail *to be ill* • **ale** *drink*

air *gas* • **e'er** *ever* • **heir** *inheritor*

aisle *passage* • **I'll** *I will* • **isle** *island*

allay *calm* • **alley** *lane* • **ally** *friend* • **alloy** *composed of two metals*

all ready *(adj.) completely prepared* • **already** *(adv.) before now*

allowed *permitted* • **aloud** *spoken*

allude *refer to* • **elude** *evade* • **illude** *cheat*

allusion *reference to* • **illusion** *false impression*

allusive *referring to* • **elusive** *evasive* • **illusive** *deceptive*

alms *charity* • **arms** *limbs*

already *(adv.) before now* • **all ready** *completely prepared*

altar *church* • **alter** *change*

alternate *first one, then the other* • **alternative** *one without the other*

alternative *one without the other* • **alternate** *first one, then the other*

altitude *height* • **attitude** *point of view*

amiable *describing a personality* • **amicable** *describing a relationship*

amicable *describing a relationship* • **amiable** *describing a personality*

amoral *without a sense of moral responsibility* • **immoral** *evil*

angel *heavenly* • **angle** *mathematics*

ant *insect* • **aunt** *relative*

ante *before* • **anti** *against* • **aunty** *relative*

anyone *(pronoun) is anyone there?* • **any one** *(adj.) I'd like any one of those girls*

apatite *mineral* • **appetite** *craving*

appetite *craving* • **apatite** *mineral*

apposite *appropriate* • **opposite** *contrary*

appraise *to judge* • **apprise** *inform* • **a prize** *a reward*

arc *curved line* • **ark** *vessel* • **arch** *building*

area *portion of land* • **aria** *opera selection*

aria *opera selection* • **area** *portion of land*

arms *limbs* • **alms** *charity*

arraign *accuse* • **arrange** *settle*

a Serb *a Yugoslav* • **acerb** *bitter*

ascent *rise* • **assent** *agree* • **accent** *speech*

assay *evaluate* • **essay** *composition*

assent *agree* • **ascent** *rise* • **accent** *speech*

assistance *help* • **assistants** *people who help*

assurance *certainty* • **insurance** *protection*

ate *did eat* • **eight** *the number*

attach *bind* • **attaché** *aide* • **attack** *assault*

attendance *act of attending* • **attendants** *people who attend*

attitude *point of view* • **altitude** *height*

aught *zero* • **ought** *should*

aunt *relative* • **ant** *insect*

aural *hearing* • **oral** *verbal*

autarchy *autocratic rule* • **autarky** *national economic self-sufficiency*

automation *electronics* • **automaton** *robot*

averse *unwilling* • **adverse** *against*

awe *fear* • **oar** *boat* • **o'er** *over* • **or** *alternative* • **ore** *mineral*

awhile *(adverb) use without 'for'* • **a while** *(noun) he stayed for a while*

axes *tools* • **axis** *line*

aye *yes* • **eye** *see* • **I** *me*

b

Incorrect	Correct
bachler	**bachelor**
backinal	**bacchanal**
backround	**background**
backwerd	**backward**
bagage	**baggage**
bagan	**began**
bage	**badge**
bagin	**begin**
baid	**bade**
baige	**beige**
baist	**baste**
bakon	**bacon**
balay	**ballet**
balence	**balance**
balistics	**ballistics**
balital	**belittle**
ballid	**ballad**
ballit	**ballot**
bamy	**balmy**
bandige	**bandage**
baner	**banner**
banista	**banister**
banjoes	**banjos**
bankrup	**bankrupt**
bankrupcy	**bankruptcy**
bannana	**banana**
baptise	**baptize**
baracks	**barracks**
barage	**barrage**

Incorrect	Correct
barate	**berate**
barbeque	**barbecue**
barell	**barrel**
bargin	**bargain**
barikade	**barricade**
barly	**barley**
barmy	**balmy**
basicly	**basically**
basik	**basic**
basiz	**basis**
bastid	**bastard**
batallian	**battalion**
batchler	**bachelor**
batray	**betray**
battry	**battery**
baught	**bought**
bawk	**balk**
baygel	**bagel**
beatle	**beetle**
beautyful	**beautiful**
becomeing	**becoming**
becon	**beacon**
becum	**become**
becuz	**because**
bedder	**better**
beever	**beaver**
beeware	**beware**
befor	**before**
beger	**beggar**

Incorrect	Correct
begile	**beguile**
beginer	**beginner**
begining	**beginning**
behavier	**behaviour**
beir	**bier**
beleaf	**belief**
beleive	**believe**
beligerant	**belligerent**
belitel	**belittle**
bely	**belie**
benafit	**benefit**
bended	**bent**
benefishal	**beneficial**
benefishery	**beneficiary**
beneith	**beneath**
benevelent	**benevolent**
benifited	**benefited**
benefitial	**beneficial**
benine	**benign**
beography	**biography**
beond	**beyond**
bequethe	**bequeath**
beray	**beret**
berbin	**bourbon**
berden	**burden**
bergler	**burglar**
berglery	**burglary**
burgular	**burglar**
berial	**burial**
beriel	**burial**
berlesk	**burlesque**
Berma	**Burma**
bernt	**burnt**
berser	**bursar**
berst	**burst**
beseige	**besiege**
beserk	**berserk**
bestyal	**bestial**
beuty	**beauty**
Bibel	**Bible**
bicect	**bisect**
biege	**beige**
bigest	**biggest**
biggamy	**bigamy**
biggot	**bigot**
bild	**build**
bilet	**billet**
biliard	**billiard**
bilion	**billion**
billyus	**bilious**
bilt	**built**
binery	**binary**
binnoculars	**binoculars**
birden	**burden**
birdy	**birdie**
bisek	**bisect**
biseps	**biceps**
biskit	**biscuit**
bisy	**busy**
biter	**bitter**
bivwak	**bivouc**
bizness	**business**
blair	**blare**
blakgard	**blackguard**

Incorrect	Correct
blamful	**blameful**
blamless	**blameless**
blankit	**blanket**
blasay	**blasé**
blasfemy	**blasphemy**
bleech	**bleach**
bleek	**bleak**
blest	**blessed**
bleve	**believe**
blite	**blight**
blith	**blithe**
blits	**blitz**
blizard	**blizzard**
blockaid	**blockade**
blok	**block**
bloter	**blotter**
blowse	**blouse**
bluf	**bluff**
blugen	**bludgeon**
blujen	**bludgeon**
boch	**botch**
boddy	**body**
boid	**bird**
boistrous	**boisterous**
bolstir	**bolster**
bom	**bomb**
bondfire	**bonfire**
bonet	**bonnet**
boney	**bony**
bonion	**bunion**
bonis	**bonus**
boodwar	**boudoir**
booey	**buoy**
bookay	**bouquet**
bookeeping	**bookkeeping**
boorzhwa	**bourgeois**
boosom	**bosom**
bord	**board**
borow	**borrow**
bost	**boast**
bosun	**boatswain**
bosy	**bossy**
botom	**bottom**
bottel	**bottle**
boundry	**boundary**
bouyant	**buoyant**
boycot	**boycott**
bracke	**brake**
brade	**braid**
bragart	**braggart**
brane	**brain**
bran-new	**brand-new**
braselet	**bracelet**
brasen	**brazen**
bravry	**bravery**
brazere	**brassiere**
breakible	**breakable**
bredth	**breadth**
breif	**brief**
brekfast	**breakfast**
brest	**breast**
brethern	**brethren**
brez	**breeze**
brigader	**brigadier**

Incorrect	Correct
brige	**bridge**
briliant	**brilliant**
Britanica	**Britannica**
brite	**bright**
Britin	**Britain**
Brittish	**British**
brocalli	**broccoli**
brokin	**broken**
brokrage	**brokerage**
bronkiel	**bronchial**
browz	**browse**
bruk	**brook**
bruzed	**bruised**
bucher	**butcher**
buckel	**buckle**
bucksome	**buxom**
Buda	**Buddha**
buety	**beauty**
bufalo	**buffalo**
bufer	**buffer**
buffay	**buffet**
bufoon	**buffoon**
buge	**budge**
bugel	**bugle**
buisness	**business**

Incorrect	Correct
bujet	**budget**
buket	**bucket**
buksom	**buxom**
buldozer	**bulldozer**
bulit	**bullet**
bulitin	**bulletin**
bullivard	**boulevard**
bullyon	**bouillon**
bumbelbee	**bumblebee**
bunglow	**bungalow**
burbin	**bourbon**
burch	**birch**
burglery	**burglary**
buriel	**burial**
buro	**bureau**
busibody	**busybody**
busness	**business**
busom	**bosom**
bussel	**bustle**
busyly	**busily**
butician	**beautician**
butiful	**beautiful**
butten	**button**
bycycle	**bicycle**
bynary	**binary**

Look-Alikes or Sound-Alikes

babble *chatter* • **bauble** *trifle* • **bubble** *as in soap bubble*

bad *no good* • **bade** *asked*

bail *security* • **bale** *bundle*

bait *a lure* • **bate** *lessen*

bald *no hair* • **bawled** *cried*

ballad *song, poem* • **ballet** *dance* • **ballot** *vote*

baloney *bunk* • **bologna** *sausage*

band *ring; orchestra* • **banned** *barred*

banns *marriage* • **bands** *groups* • **bans** *prohibits*

bard *poet* • **barred** *stopped*

bare *naked* • **bear** *carry; animal*

baring *exposing* • **bearing** *carriage; support*

baron *noble* • **barren** *empty*

base *foundation* • **bass** *deep tone*

bases *foundations; stations* • **basis** *the groundwork*

bate *lessen* • **bait** *lure*

bath *noun, sometimes verb* • **bathe** *verb only*

bathos *anticlimax* • **pathos** *that which incurs pity*

bauble *trifle* • **babble** *chatter* • **bubble** *as in soap bubble*

baud *unit of telegraph signal speed* • **bawd** *a procuress*

bawd *a procuress* • **baud** *unit of telegraph signal speed*

bawled *cried* • **bald** *no hair*

bazaar *a fair* • **bizarre** *weird*

be *exist* • **bee** *insect*

beach *shore* • **beech** *tree*

bean *vegetable* • **been** *past of be* • **bin** *box*

bear *carry; animal* • **bare** *naked*

bearing *carriage or support* • **baring** *exposing*

beat *strike* • **beet** *vegetable*

beatify *make happy; religious act* • **beautify** *make beautiful*

beau *dandy; lover* • **bow** *curved shape, as rainbow*

bee *insect* • **be** *exist*

beech *tree* • **beach** *shore*

been *past of be* • **bean** *vegetable* • **bin** *box*

beer *drink* • **bier** *coffin*

bell *rings* • **belle** *beauty*

bellow *pumps air* • **below** *under*

below *under* • **bellow** *pumps air*

berry *fruit* • **bury** *to cover*

berth *place to sleep* • **birth** *born*

beseech *beg* • **besiege** *surround, in war*

beside *at the side of* • **besides** *in addition to*

besiege *surround, in war* • **beseech** *beg*

better *more than good* • **bettor** *one who bets*

biannual *twice a year* • **biennial** *every two years*

bib *shield tied under chin* • **bibb** *nautical term, part of mast*

bid *request* • **bide** *wait*

bide *wait* • **bid** *request*

biennial *every two years* • **biannual** *twice a year*

bight *bay* • **bite** *eat*

billed *sent a bill* • **build** *construct*

bin *box* • **been** *past of be* • **bean** *vegetable*

birth *born* • **berth** *place to sleep*

bizarre *weird* • **bazaar** *a fair*

blanch *whiten* • **Blanche** *name*

Blanche *name* • **blanch** *whiten*

blew *wind; breath* • **blue** *colour*

bloc *political group* • **block** *solid piece; prevent*

boar *swine* • **bore** *drill; dull*

board *lumber or climb on* • **bored** *weary; drilled*

boarder *lodger* • **border** *edge*

bold *daring* • **bowled** *did bowl*

bolder *braver* • **boulder** *big rock*

bole *clay; tree trunk* • **boll** *weevil* • **bowl** *dish; game*

bologna *food* • **baloney** *bunk* • **Bologna** *Italian city*

born *given birth* • **borne** *carried*

borne *carried* • **born** *given birth*

burro *donkey* • **burrow** *hole, dig*

bough *tree* • **bow** *bend, yield*

bouillon *soup* • **bullion** *gold, silver*

boulder *big rock* • **bolder** *braver*

bow *curve* • **beau** *lover*

bowl *dish; game* • **bole** *clay; tree trunk* • **boll** *weevil*

bowled *did bowl* • **bold** *daring*

boy *lad* • **buoy** *a float*

braes *hillsides* • **braise** *to stew* • **brays** *utters harsh sounds* • **braze** *to solder*

braid *trim* • **brayed** *bellowed*

braise *to stew* • **braes** *hillsides* • **brays** *utters harsh sounds* • **braze** *to solder*

brake *stop* • **break** *destroy*

brays *utters harsh sounds* • **braise** *to stew* • **braes** *hillsides* • **braze** *to solder*

braze *to solder* • **braes** *hillsides* • **braise** *to stew* • **brays** *utters harsh sounds*

breach *break; violation* • **breech** *bottom*

bread *food* • **bred** *reared*

breadth *expanse* • **breath** *air inhaled* • **breathe** *to inhale and exhale*

break *destroy* • **brake** *stop*

breath *air inhaled* • **breathe** *to inhale and exhale* • **breadth** *expanse*

breathe *to inhale and exhale* • **breath** *air inhaled* • **breadth** *expanse*

brewed *liquor* • **brood** *offspring; worry*

brews *makes liquor* • **bruise** *wound*

briar *pipe wood* • **brier** *thorny bush*

bridal *wedding* • **bridle** *restrain; horse harness*

brier *thorny bush* • **briar** *pipe wood*

broach *tool; discuss* • **brooch** *a clasp*

brows *foreheads* • **browse** *read here and there*

bruit *rumour* • **brute** *savage*

bubble *as in soap bubble* • **bauble** *trifle* • **babble** *chatter*

build *construct* • **billed** *sent a bill*

bullion *gold, silver* • **bouillon** *soup*

buoy *a float* • **boy** *lad*

buccal *of the cheek* • **buckle** *fastening; warp*

burro *donkey* • **burrow** *hole, dig*

bury *put in ground* • **berry** *fruit*

but *however* • **butt** *end, object; cask* • **butte** *flat-topped hill*

buy *purchase* • **by** *near* • **bye** *indirect*

C

Incorrect	Correct
cabage	**cabbage**
cabanet	**cabinet**
cabel	**cable**
cach	**catch**
cafeine	**caffeine**
caffé	**café**
caffs	**calves**
calaco	**calico**
Calafornia	**California**
caleber	**calibre**
calender	**calendar**
caliber	**calibre**
calidiscope	**kaleidoscope**
calijun	**collision**
calipso	**calypso**
caliry	**calorie**
callamity	**calamity**
calocwiel	**colloquial**
calry	**calorie**
calsium	**calcium**
camafloge	**camouflage**
camara	**camera**
camasole	**camisole**
camelia	**camellia**
cameradery	**camaraderie**
camfer	**camphor**
campane	**campaign**
camra	**camera**
canepy	**canopy**
cannal	**canal**
cansil	**cancel**
canvis	**canvas**
canyen	**canyon**
caos	**chaos**
capashus	**capacious**
capible	**capable**
capilary	**capillary**
capitchulate	**capitulate**
capitil	**capital**
cappacity	**capacity**
caprese	**caprice**
capsel	**capsule**
capshun	**caption**
captan	**captain**
captin	**captain**
caracter	**character**
carbahidrate	**carbohydrate**
carberater	**carburettor**
cardiak	**cardiac**
cardnil	**cardinal**
carear	**career**
carefull	**careful**
careing	**caring**
caricatour	**caricature**
caried	**carried**
carit	**carat**
carm	**calm**

Incorrect	Correct	Incorrect	Correct
carmel	**caramel**	catagory	**category**
carnivul	**carnival**	catapiller	**caterpillar**
carnul	**carnal**	catar	**catarrh**
caroner	**coroner**	catastrofy	**catastrophe**
carot	**carrot**	catelogue	**catalogue**
carowse	**carouse**	cateract	**cataract**
carowz	**carouse**	cathedrel	**cathedral**
carress	**caress**	Cathlic	**Catholic**
Carribean	**Caribbean**	caticomb	**catacomb**
carrige	**carriage**	catilyon	**cotillion**
carring	**carrying**	catipult	**catapult**
cartalige	**cartilage**	catkus	**cactus**
cart blansh	**carte blanche**	cauff	**cough**
cartell	**cartel**	causious	**cautious**
cartin	**carton**	cavelcaid	**cavalcade**
cartrige	**cartridge**	caveleir	**cavalier**
cartune	**cartoon**	cavernus	**cavernous**
casarole	**casserole**	cawcus	**caucus**
cascaid	**cascade**	cawk	**caulk**
casel	**castle**	cawleflower	**cauliflower**
casheer	**cashier**	cawshun	**caution**
cashmear	**cashmere**	cawz	**cause**
cashoe	**cashew**	cazm	**chasm**
caskit	**casket**	ceder	**cedar**
casmint	**casement**	ceese	**cease**
casock	**cassock**	celabacy	**celibacy**
cassaroll	**casserole**	celebrait	**celebrate**
cassel	**castle**	celler	**cellar**
castagate	**castigate**	celophane	**cellophane**
castinet	**castanet**	celuloid	**celluloid**
casulty	**casualty**	cematary	**cemetery**
cataclism	**cataclysm**	cemicle	**chemical**

Incorrect	Correct
cenchury	**century**
cencus	**census**
centenial	**centennial**
centered	**centred**
centor	**centaur**
centrel	**central**
centrifigle	**centrifugal**
centuary	**century**
cerfue	**curfew**
cerimony	**ceremony**
certin	**certain**
chagrinned	**chagrined**
chaif	**chafe**
chaist	**chaste**
chalenge	**challenge**
champeen	**champion**
champoo	**shampoo**
chane	**chain**
chanel	**channel**
changable	**changeable**
chaplin	**chaplain**
charaty	**charity**
chare	**chair**
chariet	**chariot**
chater	**chatter**
chauffuer	**chauffeur**
chawk	**chalk**
cheder	**cheddar**
cheep	**cheap**
cheet	**cheat**
cheez	**cheese**
cheif	**chief**
Chekaslavakia	**Czechoslovakia**
chelo	**cello**
chemest	**chemist**
cherib	**cherub**
chesnut	**chestnut**
chieftin	**chieftain**
childern	**children**
chimny	**chimney**
chinchila	**chinchilla**
chints	**chintz**
chipendale	**Chippendale**
chivelrus	**chivalrous**
chizel	**chisel**
choclit	**chocolate**
choffer	**chauffeur**
chossen	**chosen**
chow	**ciao**
chow main	**chow mein**
choyce	**choice**
chrisanthemun	**chrysanthemum**
chrisen	**christen**
Christyan	**Christian**
chuby	**chubby**
chumy	**chummy**
cicle	**cycle**
ciclone	**cyclone**
cieling	**ceiling**
cigret	**cigarette**
cilynder	**cylinder**
ciment	**cement**

Incorrect	Correct
cinamon	**cinnamon**
Cinncinatti	**Cincinnati**
circal	**circle**
circomstance	**circumstance**
circuler	**circular**
circumfrence	**circumference**
circumsize	**circumcise**
cirkit	**circuit**
cist	**cyst**
citazen	**citizen**
citris	**citrus**
cival	**civil**
civlisation	**civilization**
clamer	**clamour**
clamy	**clammy**
clanish	**clannish**
clark	**clerk**
clarvoiance	**clairvoyance**
clasify	**classify**
clauz	**clause**
clearinse	**clearance**
cleek	**clique**
clense	**cleanse**
cleptamania	**kleptomania**
cleracle	**clerical**
clevige	**cleavage**
clientell	**clientele**
clif	**cliff**
cliper	**clipper**
clok	**clock**
cloke	**cloak**
cloraform	**chloroform**
closh	**cloche**
closit	**closet**
cloun	**clown**
cloyster	**cloister**
cloz	**clothes**
clozure	**closure**
clumzy	**clumsy**
coam	**comb**
cobbwebb	**cobweb**
coch	**coach**
cocksin	**coxswain**
coersion	**coercion**
cofee	**coffee**
coff	**cough**
cofin	**coffin**
cohearint	**coherent**
coinsidence	**coincidence**
cojitait	**cogitate**
colaborate	**collaborate**
colapse	**collapse**
colar	**collar**
colateral	**collateral**
coldslaw	**coleslaw**
colect	**collect**
colecter	**collector**
coleegue	**colleague**
colege	**college**
colegiate	**collegiate**
coler	**colour**
colera	**cholera**

Incorrect	Correct
colerachura	**coloratura**
Coleseum	**Colosseum**
collapsable	**collapsible**
colleck	**collect**
colledge	**college**
collegit	**collegiate**
coller	**collar**
collosal	**colossal**
Colloseum	**Coliseum**
colonaid	**colonnade**
colone	**cologne**
colouration	**coloration**
colum	**column**
colyumist	**columnist**
comemorate	**commemorate**
comendable	**commendable**
comercial	**commercial**
comftable	**comfortable**
comission	**commission**
comit	**commit**
comited	**committed**
comittee	**committee**
commedian	**comedian**
commedy	**comedy**
commen	**common**
commendible	**commendable**
commenshurite	**commensurate**
commet	**comet**
commic	**comic**
comming	**coming**
comminism	**communism**
commision	**commission**
commitee	**committee**
comodity	**commodity**
companyon	**companion**
comparitive	**comparative**
compatable	**compatible**
compatense	**competence**
compeet	**compete**
compeled	**compelled**
compell	**compel**
compermize	**compromise**
competant	**competent**
compinsashun	**compensation**
compis	**compass**
compitition	**competition**
complacate	**complicate**
complementry	**complementary**
complexshun	**complexion**
complience	**compliance**
composishun	**composition**
compoze	**compose**
compresed	**compressed**
comprible	**comparable**
compulsery	**compulsory**
comred	**comrade**
comtroller	**comptroller**
comunicate	**communicate**

Incorrect	Correct
comunity	**community**
comute	**commute**
conasseur	**connoisseur**
conceed	**concede**
concensus	**consensus**
concequence	**consequence**
concer	**concur**
conchribeaut	**contribute**
concientious	**conscientious**
concieve	**conceive**
conclaive	**conclave**
concock	**concoct**
concorse	**concourse**
concreet	**concrete**
concurense	**concurrence**
concushin	**concussion**
condem	**condemn**
condesend	**condescend**
condinsashun	**condensation**
condishun	**condition**
conduck	**conduct**
conect	**connect**
conection	**connection**
confadense	**confidence**
confederit	**confederate**
confekshinery	**confectionery**
confered	**conferred**
conferm	**confirm**
confes	**confess**
confinment	**confinement**
confligrashun	**conflagration**
confortable	**comfortable**
confrence	**conference**
Confushus	**Confucius**
congagate	**conjugate**
congell	**congeal**
congenyal	**congenial**
congradulate	**congratulate**
congrigashun	**congregation**
congrous	**congruous**
conjer	**conjure**
conjeture	**conjecture**
conker	**conquer**
connisseur	**connoisseur**
conotashun	**connotation**
conote	**connote**
conseal	**conceal**
conseat	**conceit**
conseed	**concede**
conseive	**conceive**
consentrait	**concentrate**
consentrick	**concentric**
consept	**concept**
consert	**concert**
conservitory	**conservatory**
consession	**concession**
conshunse	**conscience**

Incorrect	Correct
conshuss	**conscious**
considrable	**considerable**
consinement	**consignment**
consil	**consul**
consiliate	**conciliate**
consise	**concise**
consistant	**consistent**
consittar	**consider**
consoladate	**consolidate**
consomate	**consummate**
consoul	**console**
constible	**constable**
constilashun	**constellation**
constint	**constant**
consumtion	**consumption**
consynment	**consignment**
contajus	**contagious**
contane	**contain**
contanent	**continent**
contempry	**contemporary**
contemt	**contempt**
contemtable	**contemptible**
conterary	**contrary**
contimplate	**contemplate**
continense	**countenance**
continnualy	**continually**
continous	**continuous**
contore	**contour**
contractural	**contractual**
contrarywise	**contrariwise**
contratan	**contretemps**
contravershil	**controversial**
contraversy	**controversy**
contribeaut	**contribute**
controled	**controlled**
controll	**control**
contry	**country**
conubeal	**connubial**
conviless	**convalesce**
convilute	**convolute**
convinient	**convenient**
convirge	**converge**
convirse	**converse**
convirtable	**convertible**
convolse	**convulse**
conyak	**cognac**
coo di gra	**coup de grace**
cookoo	**cuckoo**
cookry	**cookery**
cooly	**coolly**
coopay	**coupé**
coopon	**coupon**
cooprate	**cooperate**
coper	**copper**
copeus	**copious**
Copinhagin	**Copenhagen**
cople	**couple**
coprate	**cooperate**
copyriter	**copywriter**
copywright	**copyright**
cor	**corps**

Incorrect	Correct
coral	**corral**
corcage	**corkage**
corderoy	**corduroy**
cordige	**cordage**
cordnation	**coordination**
corect	**correct**
corelate	**correlate**
coreografy	**choreography**
corespond	**correspond**
coridor	**corridor**
corigated	**corrugated**
coril	**coral**
corn-beef	**corned beef**
cornise	**cornice**
cornor	**corner**
coroborate	**corroborate**
corperal	**corporal**
corpisle	**corpuscle**
corpration	**corporation**
corraled	**corralled**
correspondance	**correspondence**
corronary	**coronary**
corsarge	**corsage**
corse	**course**
corsit	**corset**
cort	**court**
cortison	**courtesan**
cortmarshal	**courtmartial**
corz	**corps**
cosher	**kosher**
costic	**caustic**

Incorrect	Correct
cotage	**cottage**
cotin	**cotton**
counsler	**counsellor**
counterfit	**counterfeit**
countes	**countess**
courticy	**courtesy**
covrage	**coverage**
cowerd	**coward**
Cozak	**Cossack**
cozmapolitan	**cosmopolitan**
cozmic	**cosmic**
cozy	**cosy**
cozzin	**cousin**
craby	**crabby**
cradenchle	**credential**
crain	**crane**
craion	**crayon**
crak	**crack**
crakel	**crackle**
cramberry	**cranberry**
crashendo	**crescendo**
craul	**crawl**
craydal	**cradle**
creashun	**creation**
credable	**credible**
credlus	**credulous**
creedence	**credence**
creem	**cream**
creese	**crease**
creture	**creature**
crie	**cry**

Incorrect	Correct
criket	**cricket**
crimnal	**criminal**
crimsin	**crimson**
Crismas	**Christmas**
Cristian	**Christian**
cristilize	**crystallize**
critacal	**critical**
criteek	**critique**
critisise	**criticize**
crokadile	**crocodile**
crokay	**croquet**
crokete	**croquette**
cromatizm	**chromatism**
crome	**chrome**
cronic	**chronic**
croocial	**crucial**
crood	**crude**
crool	**cruel**
croopya	**croupier**
croud	**crowd**
cround	**crowned**
crowshay	**crochet**
crsanthemun	**chrysanthemum**
cruch	**crutch**
crue	**crew**
cruely	**cruelly**
crulty	**cruelty**
crum	**crumb**
crushal	**crucial**
cruzer	**cruiser**
cryed	**cried**
cubbard	**cupboard**
Cuber	**Cuba**
culcher	**culture**
culer	**colour**
cullinary	**culinary**
cultavate	**cultivate**
cumand	**command**
cumense	**commence**
cumfortable	**comfortable**
cuming	**coming**
cuning	**cunning**
cuntry	**country**
cupon	**coupon**
curancy	**currency**
curchef	**kerchief**
curent	**current**
curiculum	**curriculum**
curige	**courage**
curios	**curious**
curiousity	**curiosity**
curley	**curly**
curnel	**kernel**
currancy	**currency**
curst	**cursed**
curteous	**courteous**
custid	**custard**
custidy	**custody**
custimor	**customer**
cuver	**cover**
cuvinant	**covenant**
cwafeur	**coiffure**
cyder	**cider**

Look-Alikes or Sound-Alikes

cabal *a secret group* • **cable** *wire*

cable *wire* • **cabal** *a secret group*

cacao *tree of cocoa* • **cocoa** *chocolate*

cache *hiding-place* • **cash** *money*

caddie *golf attendant* • **caddy** *tea box*

calendar *time* • **calender** *machine to press* • **colander** *strainer*

callous *unfeeling* • **callus** *hard skin*

calm *quiet* • **cam** *machinery part*

Calvary *crucifixion* • **cavalry** *horse troops*

cam *machinery part* • **calm** *quiet*

candid *frank* • **candied** *sugared*

canon *law* • **cannon** *gun* • **canyon** *ravine*

cant *hypocrisy* • **can't** *cannot*

canvas *cloth* • **canvass** *to solicit*

capital *main, city* • **Capitol** *the building*

carat *unit of weight of diamond* • **caret** *proofreader's mark* • **carrot** *vegetable*

career *profession* • **courier** *messenger* • **currier** *leather*

carousal *orgy* • **carousel** *merry-go-round*

carousel *merry-go-round* • **carousal** *orgy*

cash *money* • **cache** *hiding-place*

cask *barrel* • **casque** *helmet*

casque *helmet* • **cask** *barrel*

cast *throw; list of actors* • **caste** *rank in society*

caster *thrower; turner* • **castor** *secretion used in medicines*

casual *easy-going* • **causal** *the cause of*

cataclasm *breakage, disruption* • **cataclysm** *great flood*

cataclysm *great flood* • **cataclasm** *breakage, disruption*

caught *did catch* • **court** *law; woo*

cease *stop* • **seize** *grab* • **seas** *bodies of water* • **sees** *observes*

cede *give up* • **seed** *flower*

ceiling *top* • **sealing** *closing*

cell *prison; unit in biology* • **sell** *opposite of buy*

cellar *basement* • **seller** *one who sells*

cemetery *graveyard* • **symmetry** *even*

censer *for incense* • **censor** *moral overseer* • **censure** *condemn*

census *population count* • **senses** *sight, touch*

cents *money* • **scents** *smells* • **sense** *brains*

cereal *food* • **serial** *in a row*

certain *sure* • **curtain** *drapery*

cession *yielding* • **session** *meeting*

champagne *wine* • **champaign** *plain*

champaign *plain* • **champagne** *wine*

charted *put on a chart* • **chartered** *rented*

chased *ran after* • **chaste** *pure*

cheap *priced low* • **cheep** *sound of young bird*

check *pause, control* • **cheque** *money* • **Czech** *nationality*

cheer *to applaud* • **jeer** *to scoff*

cheep *sound of young bird* • **cheap** *priced low*

cheque *money* • **check** *pause, control* • **Czech** *nationality*

chert *a rock* • **shirt** *garment*

chews *eats* • **choose** *select* • **Jews** *Semitic*

chic *stylish* • **chick** *young bird*

chilli *food* • **chilly** *cold* • **Chile** *country*

choir *singers* • **quire** *quantity of paper*

choler *rage* • **collar** *neckwear* • **colour** *hue*

choral *singing* • **coral** *sea life* • **corral** *animal pen*

chord *music* • **cord** *rope*

christen *baptize* • **Christian** *a believer in Christ*

Christian *a believer in Christ* • **christen** *baptize*

chute *drop* • **shoot** *fire*

Cilician *from Cilicia, a province in Asia Minor* • **Sicilian** *from Sicily, an island off and part of Italy*

cite *point out* • **sight** *see* • **site** *place*

clause *contract* • **claws** *sharp nails*

clench *close teeth* • **clinch** *to embrace; to conclude a deal*

clew *thread* • **clue** *detection*

click *noise* • **clique** *small group*

climactic *refers to climax* • **climatic** *refers to climate*

climb *ascent* • **clime** *climate*

clinch *to embrace; to conclude a deal* • **clench** *close teeth*

close *shut* • **clothes** *apparel* • **cloths** *small fabric*

coal *fire* • **kohl** *eye shadow* • **koel** *a cuckoo*

coarse *rough* • **course** *class; passage*

cockscomb *a garden plant* • **coxcomb** *fop* • **cock's comb** *comb of a cock*

cocoa *chocolate* • **cacao** *tree of cocoa*

cola *a drink* • **kola** *a nut or tree*

colander *strainer* • **calendar** *time* • **calender** *machine to press*

collage *a type of assembled fragments* • **college** *a group, as in education*

collision *crash* • **collusion** *fraud*

Colombian *of a country in South America* • **Columbian** *American*

colonel *officer* • **kernel** *seed*

colour *hue* • **collar** *neckwear* • **choler** *rage*

Columbian *American* • **Colombian** *of a country in South America*

comity *welfare* • **committee** *a group working for a definite purpose*

command *order* • **commend** *praise*

commendation *praise* • **condemnation** *denunciation*

committee *a group working for a definite purpose* • **comity** *welfare*

complacence *self-satisfaction* • **complaisance** *fulfilment of wishes of others*

complacent *pleased with oneself* • **complaisant** *desirous of pleasing*

complaisance *fulfilment of wishes of others* • **complacence** *self-satisfaction*

complaisant *desirous of pleasing* • **complacent** *pleased with oneself*

complement *make complete* • **compliment** *praise*

comprehensible *understandable* • **comprehensive** *including much*

comprehensive *including much* • **comprehensible** *understandable*

concert *musical performance* • **consort** *partner*

condemn *to find guilty* • **contemn** *to despise*

confidant *a person confided in* • **confident** *certain*

confident *certain* • **confidant** *a person confided in*

confirmer *one who ratifies* • **conformer** *one who complies with established customs*

conformer *one who complies with established customs* • **confirmer** *one who ratifies*

conscientious *painstaking* • **conscious** *aware*

conscious *aware* • **conscientious** *painstaking*

consort *partner* • **concert** *musical performance*

consul *diplomat* • **counsel** *advice* • **council** *assembly*

contemn *to despise* • **condemn** *to find guilty*

continual *repeated again and again* • **continuous** *without a break*

continuous *without a break* • **continual** *repeated again and again*

coolie *labourer* • **coolly** *in a cool manner*

coral *sea life* • **corral** *animal pen* • **choral** *singing*

core *centre* • **corps** *army* • **corpse** *body*

corespondent *paramour in divorce proceedings* • **correspondent** *one party to exchange of letters*

corporal *of the body; a soldier* • **corporeal** *material; tangible*

corporeal *material; tangible* • **corporal** *of the body; a soldier*

correspondent *one party to exchange of letters* • **corespondent** *paramour in divorce proceedings*

costume *clothes* • **custom** *habit*

council *assembly* • **counsel** *advice* • **consul** *diplomat*

councillor *member of council* • **counsellor** *adviser, lawyer*

courier *messenger* • **currier** *leather* • **career** *profession*

course *class; passage* • **coarse** *rough*

court *law; woo* • **caught** *did catch*

courtesy *manners* • **curtsy** *bow*

cousin *a relative* • **cozen** *to deceive*

coward *one who lacks courage* • **cowered** *crouched, shrank*

coxcomb *fop* • **cockscomb** *garden plant* • **cock's comb** *comb of a cock*

cozen *to deceive* • **cousin** *a relative*

creak *noise* • **creek** *stream*

crease *fold* • **kris** *cheese; dagger*

credible *believable* • **creditable** *praiseworthy*

Cretan *inhabitant of Crete* • **cretin** *a type of idiot*

crews *sailors* • **cruise** *voyage*

critic *one who criticizes* • **critique** *criticism*

crochet *a kind of knitting* • **crotchet** *a quirk; a hook*

croquet *a game played with mallets, balls* • **croquette** *a fried cake of minced food*

croquette *a fried cake of minced food* • **croquet** *a game played with mallets, balls*

cue *hint; billiards* • **queue** *line*

currant *a berry* • **current** *a stream of water, events; contemporary*

current *a stream of water, events; contemporary* • **currant** *a berry*

cygnet *a young swan* • **signet** *a seal*

cymbal *music* • **symbol** *sign*

Czech *nationality* • **check** *pause, control* • **cheque** *money*

d

Incorrect	Correct
dabate	**debate**
dable	**dabble**
dabochery	**debauchery**
dacolté	**décolleté**
dafodile	**daffodil**
dager	**dagger**
dakiri	**daiquiri**
dakron	**dacron**
dakshound	**dachshund**
dalapadate	**dilapidate**
dalia	**dahlia**
dalinkwent	**delinquent**
daluge	**deluge**
damenshin	**dimension**
damige	**damage**
danderuf	**dandruff**
dandylion	**dandelion**
danjros	**dangerous**
dary	**dairy**
dashund	**dachshund**
dat	**that**
datta	**data**
dauter	**daughter**
davelop	**develop**
daybu	**début**
dayly	**daily**
dazel	**dazzle**
debaner	**debonair**
debry	**debris**
debths	**depths**
decarate	**decorate**
decend	**descend**
decese	**decease**
deciet	**deceit**
decieve	**deceive**
decleration	**declaration**
decloté	**décolleté**
decmal	**decimal**
decon	**deacon**
decreese	**decrease**
ded	**dead**
dedecate	**dedicate**
deductable	**deductible**
deduse	**deduce**
def	**deaf**
defalt	**default**
defanitely	**definitely**
defanition	**definition**
defeet	**defeat**
defense	**defence**
defendent	**defendant**
defensable	**defensible**
defered	**deferred**
defficit	**deficit**
defiants	**defiance**
defie	**defy**
definit	**definite**
definitly	**definitely**

Incorrect	Correct
defishent	**deficient**
defiunce	**defiance**
defnite	**definite**
defrence	**deference**
defyed	**defied**
dehidrate	**dehydrate**
dekaid	**decade**
delagate	**delegate**
delemma	**dilemma**
delickacy	**delicacy**
delite	**delight**
delivry	**delivery**
delliberate	**deliberate**
dellicacy	**delicacy**
dellicatessan	**delicatessen**
dellicious	**delicious**
delt	**dealt**
deluxe	**de luxe**
demacrat	**democrat**
deminish	**diminish**
deminstrate	**demonstrate**
democrasy	**democracy**
demogogue	**demagogue**
demonstratable	**demonstrable**
demytass	**demi-tasse**
dence	**dense**
denie	**deny**
dentafrice	**dentifrice**
dentel	**dental**
dentice	**dentist**
denyal	**denial**
deoderant	**deodorant**
depature	**departure**
dependible	**dependable**
depervation	**depravation**
depo	**depot**
depravashun	**deprivation**
depresent	**depressant**
depricate	**deprecate**
deprieve	**deprive**
deps	**depths**
depudy	**deputy**
derick	**derrick**
derileck	**derelict**
derje	**dirge**
desabl	**decibel**
desastrous	**disastrous**
descover	**discover**
descrepancy	**discrepancy**
descriminate	**discriminate**
desease	**disease**
Desember	**December**
desent	**decent**
desicion	**decision**
desicrate	**desecrate**
desided	**decided**
desifer	**decipher**
desine	**design**
desireable	**desirable**
desolit	**desolate**
desparate	**desperate**
despare	**despair**
desprit	**desperate**

Incorrect	Correct	Incorrect	Correct
dessertion	**desertion**	diebetes	**diabetes**
dessicate	**desiccate**	dieing	**dying**
dessmal	**decimal**	dier	**dire**
destenation	**destination**	diference	**difference**
destribute	**distribute**	difftheria	**diphtheria**
det	**debt**	dificult	**difficult**
detale	**detail**	difrenshal	**differential**
deteck	**detect**	difuse	**diffuse**
deteriate	**deteriorate**	digestable	**digestible**
detestible	**detestable**	diging	**digging**
detterent	**deterrent**	digresive	**digressive**
dettergent	**detergent**	dijest	**digest**
dettermine	**determine**	dilect	**dialect**
devel	**devil**	diktionery	**dictionary**
devellop	**develop**	dillema	**dilemma**
devert	**divert**	dilligent	**diligent**
devide	**divide**	dillute	**dilute**
devine	**divine**	dilusion	**delusion**
devistate	**devastate**	dimensha precox	**dementia praecox**
devius	**devious**	dimminative	**diminutive**
devorce	**divorce**	dimolish	**demolish**
devulge	**divulge**	dimond	**diamond**
dexterous	**dextrous**	dinamic	**dynamic**
dezign	**design**	diner	**dinner**
dezil	**diesel**	dingy	**dinghy**
diacese	**diocese**	dinjy	**dingy**
diafram	**diaphragm**	dinning	**dining**
diarrea	**diarrhoea**	dint	**didn't**
diatishn	**dietitian**	diper	**diaper**
dicesion	**decision**	dipleat	**deplete**
dicline	**decline**	diplete	**deplete**
dicshonery	**dictionary**		

Incorrect	Correct
diplomer	**diploma**
diposit	**deposit**
direer	**diarrhoea**
dirdy	**dirty**
direcshon	**direction**
dirive	**derive**
dirogative	**derogative**
diry	**diary**
disadent	**dissident**
disagrement	**disagreement**
disallusion	**disillusion**
disalow	**disallow**
disanent	**dissonent**
disapate	**dissipate**
disaprobashun	**disapprobation**
disaray	**disarray**
disasterous	**disastrous**
disatisfy	**dissatisfy**
disbersment	**disbursement**
discod	**discard**
discomodity	**discommodity**
disconsilite	**disconsolate**
disconsurt	**disconcert**
discribe	**describe**
discrimanate	**discriminate**
discription	**description**
discurtius	**discourteous**
discwalafy	**disqualify**
disdane	**disdain**
disect	**dissect**
disegragate	**desegregate**
disemenate	**disseminate**
disent	**dissent**
disertion	**desertion**
disgize	**disguise**
disiduos	**deciduous**
disign	**design**
disimalar	**dissimilar**
disipal	**disciple**
disipline	**discipline**
disirable	**desirable**
diskus	**discuss**
dismantel	**dismantle**
dismis	**dismiss**
dismissel	**dismissal**
disociate	**dissociate**
disolution	**dissolution**
disolve	**dissolve**
disonest	**dishonest**
dispair	**despair**
disparije	**disparage**
dispensery	**dispensary**
disperporshin	**disproportion**
dispicible	**despicable**
displacment	**displacement**
disposess	**dispossess**
disposible	**disposable**
disposil	**disposal**
dispurse	**disperse**
disqualafy	**disqualify**

Incorrect	Correct	Incorrect	Correct
disrepitible	**disreputable**	docter	**doctor**
disrup	**disrupt**	doctrinare	**doctrinaire**
dissapoint	**disappoint**	docuementery	**documentary**
dissappear	**disappear**	dordel	**dawdle**
dissastrous	**disastrous**	dofin	**dauphin**
disscount	**discount**	doge	**dodge**
disscover	**discover**	dogeral	**doggerel**
disscusion	**discussion**	doledrums	**doldrums**
dissern	**discern**	dolfin	**dolphin**
dissipline	**discipline**	doller	**dollar**
disspute	**dispute**	domanere	**domineer**
distaf	**distaff**	domasile	**domicile**
distastful	**distasteful**	dominent	**dominant**
distence	**distance**	dominyon	**dominion**
disterb	**disturb**	domono	**domino**
distilation	**distillation**	doner	**donor**
distingwish	**distinguish**	dongaree	**dungaree**
distint	**distinct**	donky	**donkey**
distraut	**distraught**	dont	**don't**
distres	**distress**	donut	**doughnut**
districk	**district**	dooty	**duty**
distroy	**destroy**	dor	**door**
distruction	**destruction**	dorible	**durable**
disuade	**dissuade**	dormatory	**dormitory**
dito	**ditto**	dormint	**dormant**
divaden	**dividend**	dosege	**dosage**
divice	**device**	dosile	**docile**
divise	**devise**	dossiay	**dossier**
divoid	**devoid**	doudy	**dowdy**
divoshin	**devotion**	doue	**dough**
divurje	**diverge**	dourger	**dowager**
dizease	**disease**		

Incorrect	Correct	Incorrect	Correct
dout	**doubt**	dubbel	**double**
dovtale	**dovetail**	dubbius	**dubious**
dowery	**dowry**	Duch	**Dutch**
dragen	**dragon**	duely	**duly**
dramer	**drama**	dule	**dual**
dranege	**drainage**	dulness	**dullness**
draun	**drawn**	dulsit	**dulcet**
dred	**dread**	dum	**dumb**
dreem	**dream**	dume	**doom**
drege	**dredge**	dungin	**dungeon**
drery	**dreary**	dunse	**dunce**
dres	**dress**	dupleks	**duplex**
drie	**dry**	duplisity	**duplicity**
drifwood	**driftwood**	dupplicate	**duplicate**
dril	**drill**	durration	**duration**
dring	**drink**	durres	**duress**
drivin	**drive-in**	durring	**during**
drivway	**driveway**	duse	**deuce**
drizel	**drizzle**	dutyful	**dutiful**
drol	**droll**	duve	**dove**
dromendery	**dromedary**	duz	**does**
droping	**dropping**	duzen	**dozen**
droup	**droop**	dwarve	**dwarf**
drouze	**drowse**	dy	**die**
drownded	**drowned**	dyagnose	**diagnose**
drugery	**drudgery**	dycotomy	**dichotomy**
drugist	**druggist**	dyitery	**dietary**
drunkeness	**drunkenness**	dynasor	**dinosaur**
dryd	**dried**	dyvon	**divan**

Look-Alikes or Sound-Alikes

dairy *food* • **diary** *personal record*

dam *water* • **damn** *curse*

Dane *nationality* • **deign** *deem worthy*

days *plural of day* • **daze** *confused*

dear *loved* • **deer** *animal*

debauch *to seduce* • **debouch** *to march out*

debouch *to march out* • **debauch** *to seduce*

deceased *dead* • **diseased** *sick*

decent *good* • **descent** *go down* • **dissent** *disagreement*

decree *law* • **degree** *award from university*

defer *postpone* • **differ** *disagree*

definite *precise* • **definitive** *final*

definitive *final* • **definite** *precise*

defused *without a fuse* • **diffused** *filtered or mixed in*

deign *deem worthy* • **Dane** *nationality*

dependence *reliance on others* • **dependants** *those supported by a given person*

dependants *those supported by a given person* • **dependence** *reliance on others*

depositary *the one receiving a deposit* • **depository** *a place where anything is deposited*

deposition *testimony in writing* • **disposition** *temperament*

depository *a place where anything is deposited* • **depositary** *the one receiving a deposit*

depraved *evil* • **deprived** *forbidden*

deprecate *express disapproval* • **depreciate** *lose value*

depreciate *lose value* • **deprecate** *express disapproval*

descendant *has all the meanings of descendent* plus *functions as a noun, and means* offspring • **descendent** *falling; proceeding from an original ancestor*

descendent *falling; proceeding from an original ancestor* • **descendant** *has all the meanings of descendent* plus *functions as a noun, and means* offspring

descent *go down* • **dissent** *disagreement* • **decent** *good*

desert *dry land; abandon* • **dessert** *food*

desolate *barren* • **dissolute** *given to wasteful, pleasure-seeking activities*

dessert *food* • **desert** *dry land; abandon*

detract *take away from* • **distract** *divert*

device *a scheme, means* • **devise** *invent*

dew *moisture* • **do** *to act* • **due** *owed*

diagram *sketch* • **diaphragm** *part of body*

diary *personal record* • **dairy** *food*

die *death* • **dye** *change colour*

differ *disagree* • **defer** *postpone*

diffused *filtered or mixed in* • **defused** *without a fuse*

dinar *Yugoslav currency* • **dinner** *meal*

dine *eat* • **dyne** *a unit of force in physics*

dinner *meal* • **dinar** *Yugoslav currency*

disapprove *condemn* • **disprove** *prove wrong*

disburse *pay out* • **disperse** *break up*

discomfit *to upset another* • **discomfort** *uneasiness*

discomfort *uneasiness* • **discomfit** *to upset another*

discreet *prudent* • **discrete** *separate, disconnected*

discrete *separate, disconnected* • **discreet** *prudent*

diseased *sick* • **deceased** *dead*

disposition *temperament* • **deposition** *testimony in writing*

dissent *disagreement* • **decent** *good* • **descent** *go down*

dissolute *given to wasteful, pleasure-seeking activities* • **desolate** *barren*

distract *divert* • **detract** *take away from*

divers *several* • **diverse** *different*

diverse *different* • **divers** *several*

do *to act* • **due** *owed* • **dew** *moisture*

doe *deer* • **dough** *bread*

does *female deer (pl.)* • **doze** *nap*

done *finished* • **dun** *ask for payment; brown colour*

draft *specialized use, banking and military* • **draught** *standard use*

draught *standard use* • **draft** *specialized use, banking and military*

drawers *garment; part of chest of drawers* • **draws** *tied games, lotteries*

draws *tied games, lotteries* • **drawers** *garment; part of chest of drawers*

dual *two* • **duel** *fight*

dudgeon *anger, resentment* • **dungeon** *cell in basement of a prison*

dye *change colour* • **die** *death*

dyne *a unit of force in physics* • **dine** *eat*

e

Incorrect	Correct
earing	**earring**
earlyer	**earlier**
easly	**easily**
easment	**easement**
ebiny	**ebony**
ebulient	**ebullient**
ecconomic	**economic**
ech	**etch**
eclesiestical	**ecclesiastical**
eclips	**eclipse**
eco	**echo**
economacal	**economical**
edable	**edible**
edipus	**Oedipus**
editer	**editor**
educatable	**educable**
edyucate	**educate**
eele	**eel**
eether	**either**
efect	**effect**
efervesent	**effervescent**
effert	**effort**
eficashus	**efficacious**
efishency	**efficiency**
eg	**egg**
ege	**edge**
eger	**eager**
eggsecutive	**executive**
egle	**eagle**
egoe	**ego**
egsack	**exact**
egsactly	**exactly**
egstempiraneus	**extemporaneous**
egstink	**extinct**
egzert	**exert**
egzotic	**exotic**
eighth	**eighth**
eightteen	**eighteen**
ejeck	**eject**
eksalt	**exalt**
eksclud	**exclude**
ekscrewshiate	**excruciate**
eksist	**exist**
ekstacy	**ecstasy**
ekzonerate	**exonerate**
elagent	**elegant**
elagie	**elegy**
elament	**element**
elbo	**elbow**
eleck	**elect**
eleet	**élite**
elefent	**elephant**
elegable	**eligible**
elektristy	**electricity**
elfs	**elves**
elikser	**elixir**
elipse	**ellipse**

Incorrect	Correct
ellaberate	**elaborate**
ellaquent	**eloquent**
ellementary	**elementary**
elliminate	**eliminate**
ellisit	**elicit**
ellude	**elude**
elluminate	**illuminate**
ellusadate	**elucidate**
els	**else**
elum	**elm**
elve	**elf**
emagrint	**emigrant**
emanense	**eminence**
emarald	**emerald**
embarassed	**embarrassed**
embasador	**ambassador**
embelish	**embellish**
embezle	**embezzle**
emblim	**emblem**
embomb	**embalm**
embos	**emboss**
embrase	**embrace**
embrio	**embryo**
embroyder	**embroider**
emfasis	**emphasis**
eminate	**emanate**
emisary	**emissary**
emity	**enmity**
emmergancy	**emergency**
emmployee	**employee**
emolient	**emollient**
emoshun	**emotion**

Incorrect	Correct
empier	**empire**
emporer	**emperor**
emptyness	**emptiness**
emty	**empty**
enamerd	**enamoured**
enamy	**enemy**
encompes	**encompass**
encorporate	**incorporate**
endere	**endear**
endever	**endeavour**
endoctrinate	**indoctrinate**
endorsment	**endorsement**
enfiltrate	**infiltrate**
enforcible	**enforceable**
engeneer	**engineer**
Englind	**England**
enigetic	**energetic**
enivate	**enervate**
enny	**any**
enoble	**ennoble**
enraige	**enrage**
enrap	**enwrap**
enrapcher	**enrapture**
ensin	**ensign**
entale	**entail**
entamology	**entomology**
entatain	**entertain**
enterance	**entrance**
entier	**entire**
entise	**entice**
entree	**entry**
entreet	**entreat**

Incorrect	Correct
entreprise	**enterprise**
enuf	**enough**
enunsiate	**enunciate**
envellopes	**envelopes**
envie	**envy**
envirement	**environment**
envius	**envious**
envoke	**invoke**
envyable	**enviable**
envys	**envies**
epacure	**epicure**
epademic	**epidemic**
epasod	**episode**
epataf	**epitaph**
eppick	**epic**
eppok	**epoch**
equalibrium	**equilibrium**
equaly	**equally**
equanocks	**equinox**
equidy	**equity**
equipt	**equipped**
equivilent	**equivalent**
erace	**erase**
eratic	**erratic**
erb	**herb**
erektion	**erection**
erind	**errand**
erl	**earl**
erly	**early**
ermin	**ermine**
ernest	**earnest**
eroneus	**erroneous**
eror	**error**
erth	**earth**
Ery	**Erie**
eryudite	**erudite**
esay	**essay**
escourt	**escort**
esculator	**escalator**
esential	**essential**
Eskamo	**Eskimo**
espianoge	**espionage**
estamate	**estimate**
Ester	**Easter**
et	**ate**
eternaty	**eternity**
ethacal	**ethical**
etikete	**etiquette**
evalushun	**evolution**
evedence	**evidence**
eves	**eaves**
evning	**evening**
evry	**every**
evrywear	**everywhere**
evul	**evil**
exackly	**exactly**
exacuate	**execute**
exagarate	**exaggerate**
examanation	**examination**
exaust	**exhaust**
excede	**exceed**
excell	**excel**
excentric	**eccentric**
excercise	**exercise**

Incorrect	Correct
excert	**excerpt**
excitment	**excitement**
exessive	**excessive**
exest	**exist**
exgurshin	**excursion**
exhail	**exhale**
exhorbitant	**exorbitant**
exibit	**exhibit**
existance	**existence**
exitus	**exodus**
exma	**eczema**
expell	**expel**
expence	**expense**
expendible	**expendable**
experashun	**expiration**
experiance	**experience**
explaination	**explanation**
explative	**expletive**
explisit	**explicit**
expozure	**exposure**
expres	**express**
exray	**x-ray**
exsecutive	**executive**
exseed	**exceed**
exsellent	**excellent**
exsept	**except**
exsessive	**excessive**
exsist	**exist**
exsiteable	**excitable**
exsize	**excise**
exspense	**expense**
exsperience	**experience**
extention	**extension**
extracate	**extricate**
extracuricular	**extracurricular**
extravert	**extrovert**
extravigent	**extravagant**
extreem	**extreme**
extrordinary	**extraordinary**
exzema	**eczema**
exzile	**exile**
exzilirate	**exhilarate**
Eyetalian	**Italian**
eyether	**either**
ezy	**easy**
ezzampel	**example**

Look-Alikes or Sound-Alikes

earn *gain* • **urn** *vase*

eccentric *strange* • **acentric** *not centred*

edible *eatable* • **addible** *can be added*

edition *publishing* • **addition** *anything added*

e'er *ever* • **air** *atmosphere* • **heir** *one who inherits*

eerie *ghostly* • **Erie** *the lake* • **eery** *eerie* • **aerie** *eagle's nest*

eery *eerie* • **eerie** *ghostly* • **Erie** *the lake* • **aerie** *eagle's nest*

effect *result; to bring about* • **affect** *act or influence*

effective *impressive; operative* • **affective** *emotional*

egret *heron* • **aigrette** *ornamental plume*

eight *the number* • **ate** *did eat*

either *one of two* • **ether** *drug*

elder *refers to age and wisdom gained* • **older** *refers to age only*

elegy *poem, lament* • **eulogy** *praise*

elicit *draw out* • **illicit** *illegal*

elude *evade* • **illude** *cheat* • **allude** *refer to*

elusion *evasion, escape by deception* • **allusion** *reference to* • **illusion** *false impression*

elusive *evasive* • **allusive** *referring to* • **illusive** *deceptive*

emend *remove errors* • **amend** *change*

emerge *to come out* • **immerge** *to plunge into*

emersed *standing above* • **immersed** *plunged in liquid*

emigrant *leaves country* • **immigrant** *enters country*

emit *to send out* • **immit** *to send in*

emollient *softening* • **emolument** *profit, salary, fee*

emolument *profit, salary, fee* • **emollient** *softening*

empire *dominion* • **umpire** *referee*

enable *to make able* • **unable** *not able*

enervate *deprive of nerve or strength* • **innervate** *invigorate* • **innovate** *make changes*

enmity *hostility* • **amity** *friendship*

ensure *make certain* • **insure** *to guarantee, protect*

entomology *study of insects* • **etymology** *study of words*

envelop *to surround* • **envelope** *stationery*

epic *classic* • **epoch** *age*

epigraph *motto* • **epitaph** *inscription* • **epithet** *descriptive word added to a person's name*

equable *not varying* • **equitable** *fair*

equitable *fair* • **equable** *not varying*

era *age* • **error** *mistake*

ere *before* • **err** *to do wrong*

erect *to build* • **eruct** *to belch, cast forth*

Erie *the lake* • **eerie** *ghostly* • **eery** *eerie* • **aerie** *eagle's nest*

erotic *sexy* • **erratic** *uneven*

errand *trip* • **errant** *roving*

eruct *to belch, cast forth* • **erect** *to build*

eruption *a bursting out* • **irruption** *a bursting in*

especial *exceptional, preeminent* • **special** *particular, specific*

essay *composition* • **assay** *evaluate*

estray *(noun) anything out of its normal place* • **astray** *(adv.) out of the right place*

ether *drug* • **either** *one of two*

etymology *study of words* • **entomology** *study of insects*

eunuch *sexless* • **unique** *sole*

everyone *all persons* • **every one** *each one, considered separately, one after the other*

everything *the entire situation, viewed as one total mass* • **every thing** *each item in the given situation*

ewe *sheep* • **yew** *tree* • **you** *person*

exalt *glorify* • **exult** *rejoice*

exceed *go beyond* • **accede** *agree*

except *leave out* • **accept** *agree*

exceptionable *objectionable* • **exceptional** *out of the ordinary*

exceptional *out of the ordinary* • **exceptionable** *objectionable*

exerpt *extract* • **exert** *bring into operation*

excess *too much* • **access** *admission*

exercise *to practise* • **exorcise** *to drive away evil spirits*

exert *bring into operation* • **excerpt** *extract*

expansive *capable of stretching* • **expensive** *costly*

expensive *costly* • **expansive** *capable of stretching*

expose *to uncover* • **exposé** *an account of scandalous facts or shameful deeds*

exposé *an account of scandalous facts or shameful deeds* • **expose** *to uncover*

extant *still existing* • **extent** *range, area, volume*

eye *see* • **aye** *yes* • **I** *me*

f

Incorrect	Correct	Incorrect	Correct
fabel	**fable**	famly	**family**
fabrik	**fabric**	famus	**famous**
fabulus	**fabulous**	fancyful	**fanciful**
faceing	**facing**	fansy	**fancy**
fachewal	**factual**	fanticy	**fantasy**
fachuos	**fatuous**	fantom	**phantom**
facinate	**fascinate**	farely	**fairly**
facshun	**faction**	farenheit	**Fahrenheit**
facter	**factor**	farmacy	**pharmacy**
factery	**factory**	farse	**farce**
fadelity	**fidelity**	fase	**face**
faent	**faint**	fasetious	**facetious**
faery	**fairy**	fashial	**facial**
faim	**fame**	fashon	**fashion**
fain	**feign**	fasilitate	**facilitate**
faksimile	**facsimile**	fasinate	**fascinate**
fakt	**fact**	fasithia	**forsythia**
fakulty	**faculty**	fasodd	**façade**
fale	**fail**	fassen	**fasten**
falibel	**fallible**	fateeg	**fatigue**
falicitate	**felicitate**	fatel	**fatal**
falicy	**fallacy**	faten	**fatten**
falkin	**falcon**	fatful	**fateful**
fallse	**false**	fath	**faith**
falsafy	**falsify**	father	**farther**
falseto	**falsetto**	fathim	**fathom**
falt	**fault**	faught	**fought**
familliar	**familiar**	faverible	**favourable**
famin	**famine**	fawcet	**faucet**

Incorrect	Correct
fawl	**fall**
fayth	**faith**
feal	**feel**
feasco	**fiasco**
Febuary	**February**
fech	**fetch**
fedral	**federal**
feeblely	**feebly**
feend	**fiend**
feest	**feast**
feeture	**feature**
feild	**field**
feirce	**fierce**
fel	**fell**
fella	**fellow**
feller	**fellow**
fellony	**felony**
fellt	**felt**
femenine	**feminine**
fenobarbital	**phenobarbital**
fenomenon	**phenomenon**
fense	**fence**
fere	**fear**
ferget	**forget**
fergive	**forgive**
fernish	**furnish**
fersake	**forsake**
fertil	**fertile**
fery	**ferry**
fesable	**feasible**
festavil	**festival**
feter	**fetter**
fether	**feather**
feu	**few**
feuneril	**funeral**
feurius	**furious**
feva	**fever**
ficks	**fix**
fidle	**fiddle**
fiebrus	**fibrous**
fiel	**file**
fier	**fire**
figet	**fidget**
figger	**figure**
fikil	**fickle**
Filadelphia	**Philadelphia**
filanderer	**philanderer**
filanthropy	**philanthropy**
filately	**philately**
filay	**filet**
file	**faille**
filharmonic	**philharmonic**
fillter	**filter**
fillum	**film**
filmsy	**flimsy**
filosophy	**philosophy**
finanse	**finance**
finanshul	**financial**
finatic	**fanatic**
finese	**finesse**
fingger	**finger**
finil	**final**
finly	**finely**

Incorrect	Correct	Incorrect	Correct
fireing	**firing**	flete	**fleet**
firey	**fiery**	flie	**fly**
firlo	**furlough**	flikker	**flicker**
firment	**ferment**	flipint	**flippant**
firoshus	**ferocious**	flirtacious	**flirtatious**
firther	**further**	flite	**flight**
fishion	**fission**	flok	**flock**
fisically	**physically**	floorist	**florist**
fisiology	**physiology**	floot	**flute**
fite	**fight**	flor	**flaw**
fiting	**fitting**	flore	**floor**
fium	**fume**	floresent	**fluorescent**
flabergas	**flabbergast**	floride	**fluoride**
flache	**flake**	floris	**florist**
flachulent	**flatulent**	florish	**flourish**
flaging	**flagging**	flote	**float**
flaim	**flame**	flotila	**flotilla**
flamible	**flammable**	flouer	**flower**
flaper	**flapper**	floun	**flown**
flasid	**flaccid**	flownder	**flounder**
flatary	**flattery**	flownse	**flounce**
flaten	**flatten**	flud	**flood**
flater	**flatter**	flued	**fluid**
flaver	**flavour**	fluint	**fluent**
flaygrent	**flagrant**	flys	**flies**
flech	**flesh**	fo	**foe**
flecksible	**flexible**	fobia	**phobia**
flee	**flea**	focit	**faucet**
fleese	**fleece**	focks	**fox**
flegeling	**fledgling**	fogy	**foggy**
flem	**phlegm**	foke	**folk**
flert	**flirt**	fokil	**focal**

Incorrect	Correct
fokis	**focus**
foksel	**forecastle**
foled	**fold**
folige	**foliage**
foller	**follow**
foly	**folly**
fom	**farm**
fome	**foam**
fomer	**former**
fomula	**formula**
fon	**fawn**
fondal	**fondle**
fonetic	**phonetic**
fonics	**phonics**
fonograph	**phonograph**
fonte	**font**
fony	**phony**
forcast	**forecast**
forceable	**forcible**
forchoon	**fortune**
forck	**fork**
forclose	**foreclose**
forebid	**forbid**
fored	**forehead**
fore ever	**forever**
forfit	**forfeit**
forgone	**foregone**
forgry	**forgery**
forhead	**forehead**
forin	**foreign**
forje	**forge**
formadable	**formidable**
formaly	**formally**
forman	**foreman**
forment	**foment**
formil	**formal**
formost	**foremost**
forrest	**forest**
forrum	**forum**
forsee	**foresee**
forsight	**foresight**
fortatude	**fortitude**
forteen	**fourteen**
fosfate	**phosphate**
fosforescence	**phosphorescence**
fosforus	**phosphorus**
fosil	**fossil**
foth	**forth**
foto	**photo**
fountin	**fountain**
fourty	**forty**
foward	**forward**
fownd	**found**
fraim	**frame**
frale	**frail**
frase	**phrase**
frate	**freight**
fraygrince	**fragrance**
freek	**freak**
Freid	**Freud**
frekel	**freckle**
frend	**friend**
frequincy	**frequency**

Incorrect	Correct	Incorrect	Correct
freshin	**freshen**	fugative	**fugitive**
fricasee	**fricassee**	fuge	**fugue**
fricshin	**friction**	fuje	**fudge**
frier	**friar**	fullfil	**fulfil**
frinje	**fringe**	fumbil	**fumble**
frite	**fright**	funcshin	**function**
friternel	**fraternal**	fundimental	**fundamental**
frivlous	**frivolous**	funel	**funnel**
frojalent	**fraudulent**	funeril	**funeral**
frok	**frock**	fungis	**fungus**
fronteersman	**frontiersman**	funy	**funny**
		furlow	**furlough**
frontspiece	**frontispiece**	furm	**firm**
frosen	**frozen**	furnature	**furniture**
frought	**fraught**	fury	**furry**
froun	**frown**	fusalage	**fuselage**
frugl	**frugal**	fusha	**fuchsia**
fruntil	**frontal**	fust	**first**
frutful	**fruitful**	futball	**football**
Fryday	**Friday**	futere	**future**
fued	**feud**	futil	**futile**
fuedal	**feudal**	fyancy	**fiancé**

Look-Alikes or Sound-Alikes

facet *side* • **faucet** *tap*

facility *skill* • **felicity** *happiness*

faerie *obsolete spelling of fairy, meaning enchantment* • **fairy** *a supernatural being* • **ferry** *boat*

fain *glad* • **feign** *invent*

faint *weak* • **feint** *pretend*

fair *just* • **fare** *pay for travel*

fairy *a supernatural being* • **faerie** *obsolete spelling of fairy, meaning enchantment* • **ferry** *boat*

faker *fraud* • **fakir** *Indian ascetic*

fantasy *a far-fetched imaginary idea* • **phantasy** *same as fantasy, more archaic*

farther *refers to physical distance* • **further** *refers to extent or degree*

fatal *deadly* • **fateful** *of very great importance*

fate *destiny* • **fête** *festival*

fateful *of very great importance* • **fatal** *deadly*

faun *rural deity* • **fawn** *be servile; young deer*

fays *fairies* • **faze** *worry* • **phase** *stage*

feint *pretend* • **faint** *weak*

felicity *happiness* • **facility** *skill*

ferment *yeast* • **foment** *incite*

fiancé *engaged man* • **finance** *money*

fiend *monster* • **friend** *companion*

filing *put in order* • **filling** *to make full*

finale *the end* • **finally** *at last* • **finely** *excellently*

find *locate* • **fined** *penalty*

fineness *being fine* • **finesse** *subtle skill*

fir *tree* • **fur** *hair of animal*

fiscal *money* • **physical** *body*

fisher *one who fishes* • **fissure** *split*

flagrant *glaring* • **fragrant** *nice odour*

flair *aptitude* • **flare** *burn*

flaunt *ostentatious display* • **flout** *reject contemptuously*

flea *insect* • **flee** *run away*

flèche *a spire* • **flesh** *meat*

flesh *meat* • **flèche** *a spire*

flew *did fly* • **flu** *influenza* • **flue** *chimney*

floe *ice* • **flow** *drift*

flour *food* • **flower** *plant*

flout *reject contemptuously* • **flaunt** *ostentatious display*

flow *drift* • **floe** *ice*

fogy *old-fashioned* • **foggy** *blurred*

foment *incite* • **ferment** *yeast*

fondling *caressing* • **foundling** *deserted infant*

for *on behalf of* • **four** *number* • **fore** *front*

forego *precede* • **forgo** *do without*

foreword *introduction* • **forward** *move ahead*

formally *conventionally* • **formerly** *before now*

fort *military* • **forte** *strong point* • **fought** *did fight*

forth *forward* • **fourth** *number*

foul *dirty; unfair* • **fowl** *bird*

foundling *deserted infant* • **fondling** *caressing*

franc *French money* • **frank** *blunt*

Frances *girl* • **Francis** *boy* • **France's** *of France*

frays *battles* • **phrase** *words*

frees *sets free* • **freeze** *cold* • **frieze** *cloth or ornament*

frenetic *frantic* • **phrenetic** *insane*

friend *companion* • **fiend** *monster*

funeral *a ceremony for the dead* • **funereal** *mournful*

funereal *mournful* • **funeral** *a ceremony for the dead*

fur *hair of animal* • **fir** *tree*

further *refers to extent or degree* • **farther** *refers to physical distance*

g

Incorrect	Correct
gaberdeen	**gabardine**
gage	**gauge**
gaget	**gadget**
gail	**gale**
gailic	**gallic**
gaim	**game**
galacksy	**galaxy**
galary	**gallery**
galent	**gallant**
galin	**gallon**
galip	**gallop**
galows	**gallows**
gambul	**gamble**
gammit	**gamut**
gangreen	**gangrene**
garantee	**guarantee**
gararge	**garage**
garbige	**garbage**
gard	**guard**
gardin	**garden**
gardner	**gardener**
garilus	**garrulous**
garit	**garret**
garlick	**garlic**
gasalene	**gasoline**
gasha	**geisha**
gaskit	**gasket**
gasseous	**gaseous**
gastly	**ghastly**
gatare	**guitar**
gawdy	**gaudy**
gawse	**gauze**
gaz	**gas**
gazel	**gazelle**
gazet	**gazette**
geep	**jeep**
geer	**gear**
geesha	**geisha**
geetar	**guitar**
geneology	**genealogy**
genrally	**generally**
genrus	**generous**
gentelman	**gentleman**
gentlely	**gently**
genuwine	**genuine**
genyus	**genius**
gergul	**gurgle**
gerl	**girl**
germain	**germane**
Germin	**German**
gescher	**gesture**
gess	**guess**
gest	**guest**
getto	**ghetto**
gidance	**guidance**
gide	**guide**
gidy	**giddy**
gient	**giant**

Incorrect	Correct
gigal	**giggle**
giggolo	**gigolo**
gilless	**guileless**
gimick	**gimmick**
giminasium	**gymnasium**
ginacology	**gynaecology**
ginee	**guinea**
gingam	**gingham**
girdal	**girdle**
gise	**guise**
givaway	**giveaway**
giy	**guy**
glair	**glare**
glajer	**glazier**
glamerus	**glamorous**
glanse	**glance**
glas	**glass**
glashul	**glacial**
gleem	**gleam**
glidder	**glider**
glimer	**glimmer**
glimse	**glimpse**
gliserin	**glycerine**
gliter	**glitter**
globle	**global**
glorafy	**glorify**
glosary	**glossary**
glume	**gloom**
glutin	**glutton**
goble	**gobble**
goblit	**goblet**
goch	**gauche**
gode	**goad**
godess	**goddess**
gofer	**gopher**
gole	**goal**
gon	**gone**
gondala	**gondola**
gord	**gourd**
Gorgia	**Georgia**
gorgous	**gorgeous**
gormet	**gourmet**
gosamer	**gossamer**
gosip	**gossip**
gosspel	**gospel**
gost	**ghost**
gote	**goat**
goun	**gown**
govener	**governor**
govenment	**government**
graditude	**gratitude**
gradjel	**gradual**
graf	**graph**
graid	**grade**
gramer	**grammar**
gran	**grand**
granaid	**grenade**
grandaughter	**granddaughter**
grandur	**grandeur**
grane	**grain**
gras	**grass**
grashus	**gracious**
gravaty	**gravity**

Incorrect	Correct	Incorrect	Correct
gravle	**gravel**	grose	**gross**
grayhound	**greyhound**	grosry	**grocery**
graysful	**graceful**	grotesk	**grotesque**
greatful	**grateful**	grovil	**grovel**
gredy	**greedy**	gruje	**grudge**
greif	**grief**	guage	**gauge**
greive	**grieve**	gud	**good**
greivence	**grievance**	guidence	**guidance**
grene	**green**	gullable	**gullible**
grete	**greet**	guner	**gunner**
grewsome	**gruesome**	guse	**goose**
greze	**grease**	guter	**gutter**
grile	**grille**	guterul	**gutteral**
grimas	**grimace**	guverment	**government**
groap	**grope**	guvnor	**governor**
grone	**groan**	guyser	**geyser**
groop	**group**	gypsim	**gypsum**

Look-Alikes or Sound-Alikes

gage *security* • **gauge** *measure*

gait *walk* • **gate** *door*

gallstone *pertains to medicine* • **goldstone** *pertains to mineralogy*

gamble *bet* • **gambol** *frolic*

gamin *a street urchin* • **gammon** *meat*

gaol *prison* • **goal** *destination*

gat *obsolete past tense of get* • **ghat** *a pass through a mountain chain*

geezer *old man* • **geyser** *hot spring*

genius *brilliant* • **genus** *class*

genteel *polite* • **gentle** *tame* • **gentile** *non-Jewish*

gesture *move* • **jester** *clown*

geyser *hot spring* • **geezer** *old man*

ghat *a pass through a mountain chain* • **gat** *obsolete past tense of get*

gibe *to sneer at* • **jibe** *gibe* • **gybe** *in sailing, to swing from side to side*

gild *gold cover* • **guild** *association*

gilt *gold* • **guilt** *lawbreaking*

glacier *ice formation* • **glazier** *glassmaker*

gloom *sad, dismal atmosphere* • **glume** *botanical term*

glume *botanical term* • **gloom** *sad, dismal atmosphere*

gluten *substance found in flour of wheat and other grains* • **glutton** *a person who eats to excess*

glutton *a person who eats to excess* • **gluten** *substance found in flour of wheat and other grains*

gnu *animal* • **knew** *did know* • **new** *not old*

goldstone *pertains to mineralogy* • **gallstone** *pertains to medicine*

gorilla *ape* • **guerrilla** *resistance fighter*

grate *bars; grind* • **great** *large*

grease *oil or unctuous matter* • **Greece** *country*

grip *grasp* • **gripe** *complain* • **grippe** *disease*

grisly *ghastly* • **gristly** *full of gristle* • **grizzly** *greyish*

groan *moan* • **grown** *mature*

guerrilla *resistance fighter* • **gorilla** *ape*

guessed *did guess* • **guest** *visitor*

guild *association* • **gild** *gold cover*

guilt *lawbreaker* • **gilt** *gold*

guise *manner* • **guys** *men*

gybe *in sailing, to swing from side to side* • **gibe** *to sneer at* • **jibe** *gibe*

h

Incorrect	Correct
habadasher	**haberdasher**
habichawate	**habituate**
habillitate	**habilitate**
hach	**hatch**
hadick	**haddock**
hae	**hay**
haf	**half**
hagerd	**haggard**
hagil	**haggle**
hainus	**heinous**
hairbrained	**harebrained**
hairloom	**heirloom**
hait	**hate**
halaluyah	**hallelujah**
Halaween	**Halloween**
halfs	**halves**
halow	**hallow**
halsion	**halcyon**
halusinate	**hallucinate**
hamberger	**hamburger**
hamer	**hammer**
hamlit	**hamlet**
handel	**handle**
handycap	**handicap**
hanful	**handful**
hangkerchif	**handkerchief**
hansome	**handsome**
hant	**haunt**
hapin	**happen**
happly	**happily**
haradin	**harridan**
harange	**harangue**
harber	**harbour**
harboild	**hard-boiled**
hardning	**hardening**
haried	**harried**
Harlacwin	**Harlequin**
harmoenyus	**harmonious**
harnis	**harness**
harrass	**harass**
harth	**hearth**
harty	**hearty**
hasard	**hazard**
hasen	**hasten**
hasienda	**hacienda**
hasle	**hassle**
hatchit	**hatchet**
Hawayi	**Hawaii**
hawse	**horse**
hiyena	**hyena**
haylo	**halo**
hayrim	**harem**
hayvin	**haven**
hazil	**hazel**
headake	**headache**
headinist	**hedonist**
headress	**headdress**
heartally	**heartily**

Incorrect	Correct	Incorrect	Correct
hecktic	**hectic**	herredity	**heredity**
hed	**head**	herron	**heron**
hede	**heed**	her's	**hers**
heep	**heap**	herse	**hearse**
heet	**heat**	hertofore	**heretofore**
heffer	**heifer**	hesatate	**hesitate**
heighth	**height**	hetagenius	**heterogeneous**
heirarchy	**hierarchy**	hethin	**heathen**
heje	**hedge**	heve	**heave**
hekil	**heckle**	heven	**heaven**
heksigon	**hexagon**	hevy	**heavy**
hel	**hell**	hibonate	**hibernate**
hellicopter	**helicopter**	hibread	**hybrid**
hellmit	**helmet**	hibrow	**highbrow**
helo	**hello**	hich	**hitch**
helth	**health**	hiden	**hidden**
hemaglobin	**haemoglobin**	hideus	**hideous**
hemesphere	**hemisphere**	hidrafobia	**hydrophobia**
hemmorage	**haemorrhage**	hidranja	**hydrangea**
hemmoroids	**haemorrhoids**	hidraulic	**hydraulic**
hena	**henna**	hidrint	**hydrant**
hensfourth	**henceforth**	hidrogen	**hydrogen**
heratige	**heritage**	hiensite	**hindsight**
herbashus	**herbaceous**	hifen	**hyphen**
herdel	**hurdle**	hight	**height**
herild	**herald**	hikery	**hickory**
hering	**herring**	hillarius	**hilarious**
herisy	**heresy**	hinderance	**hindrance**
herl	**hurl**	hiness	**highness**
hermatage	**hermitage**	hinj	**hinge**
heros	**heroes**	hipadermic	**hypodermic**
		hipertension	**hypertension**

Incorrect	Correct
hipnotist	**hypnotist**
hipocrite	**hypocrite**
hipopotimis	**hippopotamus**
hirarchy	**hierarchy**
hirling	**hireling**
hiroglific	**hieroglyphic**
histeria	**hysteria**
histry	**history**
hoby	**hobby**
hocky	**hockey**
hojpoj	**hodgepodge**
hoks	**hoax**
holesale	**wholesale**
holesome	**wholesome**
holindaze	**hollandaise**
hollicust	**holocaust**
holliday	**holiday**
holow	**hollow**
holyness	**holiness**
hom	**home**
homaker	**homemaker**
homaside	**homicide**
homegeneous	**homogeneous**
homly	**homely**
hommage	**homage**
homsted	**homestead**
honerable	**honourable**
honeydo	**honeydew**
honist	**honest**
honny	**honey**

Incorrect	Correct
honrary	**honorary**
hornt	**haunt**
hoo	**who**
hoove	**hoof**
hopeing	**hoping**
horafyd	**horrified**
horemone	**hormone**
horenjus	**horrendous**
horible	**horrible**
horizen	**horizon**
hornit	**hornet**
horra	**horror**
horrorscope	**horoscope**
horsey	**horsy**
horspital	**hospital**
hortaculcher	**horticulture**
horty	**haughty**
hosh	**harsh**
hospatol	**hospital**
hostige	**hostage**
hostyle	**hostile**
hottel	**hotel**
houshold	**household**
houswife	**housewife**
houzing	**housing**
hovist	**harvest**
howel	**howl**
hownd	**hound**
howzes	**houses**
hoy polloy	**hoi polloi**
hoyst	**hoist**
hoze	**hose**

Incorrect	Correct	Incorrect	Correct
hoziery	**hosiery**	huricane	**hurricane**
hud	**hood**	hurridly	**hurriedly**
hudel	**huddle**	husle	**hustle**
huf	**hoof**	huvel	**hovel**
huk	**hook**	huver	**hover**
humer	**humour**	huzbind	**husband**
humilliate	**humiliate**	huzy	**hussy**
huming	**humming**	hyatis	**hiatus**
humrus	**humorous**	hygene	**hygiene**
hunderd	**hundred**	hymnil	**hymnal**
hungar	**hunger**	hypacrite	**hypocrite**
hungary	**hungry**	hypatheticle	**hypothetical**
huray	**hurray**	hypocracy	**hypocrisy**

Look-Alikes or Sound-Alikes

hail *salute; ice* • **hale** *hearty*

hair *on head* • **hare** *rabbit*

haircut *the process of cutting the hair* • **haricot** *bean; stew*

hale *hearty* • **hail** *salute; ice*

hall *room* • **haul** *pull in*

hallow *to make holy* • **halo** *circle of light around head to show saintliness* • **hollow** *empty inside*

handsome *looks* • **hansom** *cab*

hangar *shelter* • **hanger** *clothes holder*

haricot *bean; stew* • **haircut** *the process of cutting the hair*

hart *stag* • **heart** *body*

haunch *buttocks* • **hunch** *a guess, conjecture*

hay *dried grass eaten by cattle* • **hey!** *an exclamation*

heal *mend* • **heel** *of foot* • **he'll** *he will*

hear *with the ear* • **here** *this place*

heard *did hear* • **herd** *animals*

heaume *helmet* • **home** *a house*

heir *inheritor* • **air** *atmosphere* • **e'er** *ever*

hence *from this time or place* • **thence** *from that time or place*

heroin *drug* • **heroine** *female hero*

hew *chop* • **hue** *colour* • **Hugh** *name*

hey! *an exclamation* • **hay** *dried grass eaten by cattle*

higher *taller* • **hire** *employ*

him *he* • **hymn** *song*

hoar *white with age or frost* • **whore** *prostitute*

hoard *collect* • **horde** *swarm*

hoarse *harsh* • **horse** *animal*

hoes *digs* • **hose** *stockings*

hole *opening* • **whole** *complete*

holey *having holes* • **holy** *religious* • **wholly** *fully*

holiday *a day of exemption from work* • **holy day** *a religious feast day*

hollow *empty inside* • **hallow** *to make holy* • **halo** *circle of light around head to show saintliness*

holy day *a religious feast day* • **holiday** *a day of exemption from work*

home *a house* • **heaume** *helmet*

homogeneous *of the same character, essentially alike* • **homogenous** *of common origin*

homogenous *of common origin* • **homogeneous** *of the same character, essentially alike*

hoop *circle* • **whoop** *yell*

hospitable *friendly* • **hospital** *for the sick*

hour *time* • **our** *belongs to us*

hue *colour* • **hew** *chop* • **Hugh** *name*

human *of man* • **humane** *kind*

humorous *funny* • **humerus** *bone*

hunch *a guess, conjecture* • **haunch** *buttocks*

hymn *song* • **him** *he*

hypercritical *over-critical* • **hypocritical** *pretending to be what one is not*

i

Incorrect	Correct
iadine	**iodine**
ibeks	**ibex**
iceing	**icing**
ich	**itch**
ideel	**ideal**
ideer	**idea**
idendicle	**identical**
identafy	**identify**
idget	**idiot**
idiet	**idiot**
idiology	**ideology**
idiosyncracy	**idiosyncrasy**
idium	**idiom**
idollater	**idolater**
idylic	**idyllic**
idz	**ides**
iern	**iron**
ignamineus	**ignominious**
ignerant	**ignorant**
ignor	**ignore**
igwana	**iguana**
igzasprate	**exasperate**
ikon	**icon**
ikonoclass	**iconoclast**
ikthiology	**ichthyology**
iland	**island**
ile	**isle**
ilegal	**illegal**
ilegible	**illegible**
iliterate	**illiterate**
illagitimate	**illegitimate**
illiad	**Iliad**
illisit	**illicit**
ilness	**illness**
ilogigal	**illogical**
ilujun	**illusion**
iluminate	**illuminate**
ilustrate	**illustrate**
imaculate	**immaculate**
imadgine	**imagine**
imaginible	**imaginable**
imagrint	**immigrant**
imatation	**imitation**
imaterial	**immaterial**
imature	**immature**
imbicile	**imbecile**
imbiew	**imbue**
imeasureable	**immeasurable**
imediate	**immediate**
imense	**immense**
imige	**image**
iminint	**imminent**
immagination	**imagination**
immemrable	**immemorable**
immesh	**enmesh**
imobil	**immobile**

Incorrect	Correct
imoral	**immoral**
imortil	**immortal**
impare	**impair**
imparshal	**impartial**
impashent	**impatient**
impashoned	**impassioned**
impass	**impasse**
impaterbable	**imperturbable**
impatus	**impetus**
impech	**impeach**
impecible	**impeccable**
impeed	**impede**
impeerial	**imperial**
impell	**impel**
impenitrible	**impenetrable**
impetent	**impotent**
impicunius	**impecunious**
impinje	**impinge**
impius	**impious**
implament	**implement**
implaquable	**implacable**
implie	**imply**
implisit	**implicit**
imployee	**employee**
importence	**importance**
imposibility	**impossibility**
imprasario	**impresario**
impres	**impress**
impreshin	**impression**
impromtu	**impromptu**
improvment	**improvement**

Incorrect	Correct
impuin	**impugn**
impyaty	**impiety**
imune	**immune**
inable	**enable**
inabt	**inapt**
inacceptable	**unacceptable**
inain	**inane**
inate	**innate**
inaugarate	**inaugurate**
inavoidable	**unavoidable**
inbalance	**imbalance**
imbieb	**imbibe**
incalcable	**incalculable**
incarnit	**incarnate**
incesint	**incessant**
inchant	**enchant**
inchoir	**enquire**
incidently	**incidentally**
incipid	**insipid**
inclanation	**inclination**
inclemit	**inclement**
inclood	**include**
inclosher	**enclosure**
incogneto	**incognito**
incombent	**incumbent**
incondecent	**incandescent**
incorijible	**incorrigible**
incorperate	**incorporate**
incourage	**encourage**
incrament	**increment**
incredable	**incredible**

Incorrect	Correct	Incorrect	Correct
increse	**increase**	inersha	**inertia**
incroch	**encroach**	inervate	**innervate**
incured	**incurred**	inevatable	**inevitable**
incuring	**incurring**	inexrable	**inexorable**
incyclopedia	**encyclopedia**	infadelaty	**infidelity**
indago	**indigo**	infalible	**infallible**
indalent	**indolent**	infanitly	**infinitely**
indefensable	**indefensible**	infecshun	**infection**
indekerus	**indecorous**	infent	**infant**
indeks	**index**	infered	**infrared**
indelable	**indelible**	inferier	**inferior**
independant	**independent**	infermary	**infirmary**
indesent	**indecent**	infermashun	**information**
indesirable	**undesirable**	infimous	**infamous**
indetted	**indebted**	infinative	**infinitive**
indiferent	**indifferent**	infincy	**infancy**
indijinus	**indigenous**	infiriate	**infuriate**
indiketive	**indicative**	inflamable	**inflammable**
inditement	**indictment**	inflashin	**inflation**
individuly	**individually**	inflеckshun	**inflection**
indocternate	**indoctrinate**	influinse	**influence**
indomnitable	**indomitable**	inforce	**enforce**
indowment	**endowment**	infrence	**inference**
inducment	**inducement**	infur	**infer**
indurance	**endurance**	infuze	**infuse**
industral	**industrial**	ingagement	**engagement**
Indyan	**Indian**	ingection	**injection**
inefable	**ineffable**	ingine	**engine**
ineficashus	**inefficacious**	Inglish	**English**
iner	**inner**	ingrachiate	**ingratiate**
		ingrave	**engrave**
		ingreedient	**ingredient**

Incorrect	Correct
inhabatint	**inhabitant**
inhabition	**inhibition**
inhail	**inhale**
inhanse	**enhance**
inherrit	**inherit**
inishal	**initial**
injary	**injury**
injeanius	**ingenius**
injery	**injury**
injoyment	**enjoyment**
injustise	**injustice**
inlighten	**enlighten**
innacurate	**inaccurate**
innapropriate	**inappropriate**
innaugurate	**inaugurate**
innauspicious	**inauspicious**
innebreate	**inebriate**
innechative	**initiative**
inneficient	**inefficient**
innoculate	**inoculate**
inocense	**innocence**
inocuous	**innocuous**
inordinant	**inordinate**
inormous	**enormous**
inovate	**innovate**
inpersonal	**impersonal**
inpolite	**impolite**
inquier	**inquire**
inrich	**enrich**
insalate	**insulate**

Incorrect	Correct
insalent	**insolent**
insanaty	**insanity**
inscrewtable	**inscrutable**
inseck	**insect**
insendery	**incendiary**
insentive	**incentive**
inseprable	**inseparable**
insest	**incest**
insident	**incident**
insied	**inside**
insinerator	**incinerator**
insipient	**incipient**
insipordinate	**insubordinate**
insise	**incise**
insistant	**insistent**
insite	**insight**
insolluble	**insoluble**
insparation	**inspiration**
instagate	**instigate**
instatute	**institute**
insted	**instead**
instense	**instance**
instink	**instinct**
instintaneus	**instantaneous**
instrament	**instrument**
insufrable	**insufferable**
intagrate	**integrate**
intamate	**intimate**
intamediate	**intermediate**
intangle	**entangle**

Incorrect	Correct
intanjible	**intangible**
integeral	**integral**
intelectual	**intellectual**
intelegance	**intelligence**
intemprate	**intemperate**
intensafy	**intensify**
intenshun	**intention**
intercep	**intercept**
intercorse	**intercourse**
interduce	**introduce**
interferance	**interference**
interlewd	**interlude**
intermitent	**intermittent**
internul	**internal**
interpalate	**interpolate**
interpet	**interpret**
interrest	**interest**
intersede	**intercede**
intersession	**intercession**
interupt	**interrupt**
intervue	**interview**
inthusiasm	**enthusiasm**
intifere	**interfere**
intoragate	**interrogate**
intoxacate	**intoxicate**
intracacy	**intricacy**
intreeg	**intrigue**
intresting	**interesting**
intrist	**interest**
inuendo	**innuendo**
inurt	**inert**
invallid	**invalid**
invazhun	**invasion**
invegel	**inveigle**
invenerate	**inveterate**
investagate	**investigate**
invigerate	**invigorate**
invironment	**environment**
invit	**invite**
invizable	**invisible**
invoise	**invoice**
inwerd	**inward**
iradesense	**iridescence**
irational	**irrational**
iredeemable	**irredeemable**
iregular	**irregular**
irelevance	**irrelevance**
iresistable	**irresistible**
iresistible	**irresistible**
iresponsible	**irresponsible**
irevocable	**irrevocable**
irigate	**irrigate**
iritable	**irritable**
irrascible	**irascible**
irregardless	**regardless**
irrelentless	**relentless**
irrevelant	**irrelevant**
isalate	**isolate**
isatope	**isotope**
isberg	**iceberg**
ise	**ice**
ishue	**issue**

Incorrect	Correct	Incorrect	Correct
ishuence	**issuance**	ivey	**ivy**
ismus	**isthmus**	Izlam	**Islam**
itim	**item**	Izland	**Iceland**
ivary	**ivory**	Izrael	**Israel**

Look-Alikes or Sound-Alikes

idle *inactive* • **idol** *false god* • **idyll** *simple pastoral scene*

I'll *I will* • **aisle** *passage* • **isle** *island*

illegible *unreadable* • **ineligible** *unqualified*

illicit *illegal* • **elicit** *draw out*

illude *cheat* • **allude** *refer to* • **elude** *evade*

illusion *false impression* • **elusion** *evasion, escape by deception* • **allusion** *reference to*

illusive *deceptive* • **allusive** *referring to* • **elusive** *evasive*

imbrue *moisten, especially with blood* • **imbue** *permeate, colour deeply*

imbue *permeate, colour deeply* • **imbrue** *moisten, especially with blood*

immerge *to plunge into* • **emerge** *to come out*

immersed *plunged in* • **emersed** *standing out*

immigrant *enters country* • **emigrant** *leaves country*

imminent *about to happen* • **immanent** *inherent*

immit *to send in* • **emit** *to send out*

immoral *evil* • **amoral** *without a sense of moral responsibility*

immunity *exemption from duty; power to resist disease* • **impunity** *exemption from punishment or harm*

impassable *closed* • **impassible** *incapable of being hurt* • **impossible** *not possible*

impostor *pretender* • **imposture** *deception*

impunity *exemption from punishment or harm* • **immunity** *exemption from duty; power to resist disease*

in *(prep.) on the inside* • **inn** *hotel*

inane *pointless* • **insane** *mad*

incidents *happenings* • **incidence** *occurrence*

incipient *beginning to exist* • **insipient** *unwise*

incite *stir up* • **insight** *keen understanding*

indiscreet *unwise* • **indiscrete** *unseparated*

inditement *act of composition* • **indictment** *written accusation*

ineligible *not qualified* • **illegible** *unreadable*

inequity *injustice* • **iniquity** *wickedness*

ingenious *original* • **ingenuous** *innocent*

inn *hotel* • **in** *(prep.) on the inside*

innervate *invigorate* • **innovate** *make changes* • **enervate** *deprive of strength*

insane *mad* • **inane** *pointless*

insert *to put in* • **inset** *that which is set in*

insight *keen understanding* • **incite** *stir up*

insipient *unwise* • **incipient** *beginning to exist*

insulate *to place in a detached situation* • **insolate** *to expose to the sun*

insurance *protection* • **assurance** *certainty*

insure *guarantee, protect* • **ensure** *make certain*

intense *in an extreme degree* • **intents** *purposes*

intern *an inmate; to detain* • **inturn** *an inward turn or bend*

internment *state of being detained or held* • **interment** *burial*

interpellate *to question a minister or executive officer* • **interpolate** *to alter or insert new matter*

interpolate *to alter or insert new matter* • **interpellate** *to question a minister or executive officer*

intestate *without a will* • **interstate** *between states* • **intrastate** *within state*

inturn *an inward turn or bend* • **intern** *an inmate; to detain*

irrelevant *not pertinent* • **irreverent** *disrespectful*

irruption *a bursting in* • **eruption** *a bursting out*

isle *island* • **aisle** *passage* • **I'll** *I will*

it's *it is* • **its** *belonging to it*

j

Incorrect	Correct
jackel	**jackal**
jacknife	**jackknife**
jagantic	**gigantic**
jaged	**jagged**
jagwar	**jaguar**
jaid	**jade**
jakass	**jackass**
jaket	**jacket**
jale	**jail**
janator	**janitor**
janetic	**genetic**
Januwery	**January**
Jappenese	**Japanese**
jardineer	**jardiniere**
jargin	**jargon**
jawndis	**jaundice**
jaz	**jazz**
jazmin	**jasmine**
jeanius	**genius**
jeanyal	**genial**
jelatin	**gelatine**
jellus	**jealous**
jely	**jelly**
jentile	**gentile**
jepordy	**jeopardy**
jerney	**journey**
jersy	**jersey**
jeryatricks	**geriatrics**
jest	**just**
jetison	**jettison**
jety	**jetty**
jewelry	**jewellery**
jewls	**jewels**
Jezuit	**Jesuit**
jibbet	**gibbet**
jieb	**jibe**
jiger	**jigger**
jilopy	**jalopy**
jimy	**jimmy**
jinjer	**ginger**
jip	**gyp**
jipsee	**gypsy**
jiraf	**giraffe**
jirascope	**gyroscope**
jiterbug	**jitterbug**
jober	**jobber**
jodpurs	**jodhpurs**
jokey	**jockey**
jokker	**joker**
jokular	**jocular**
joly	**jolly**
jondarm	**gendarme**
joobilunt	**jubilant**
joodishal	**judicial**
jools	**jewels**
joonyer	**junior**
joorisdicshun	**jurisdiction**
joose	**juice**

Incorrect	Correct	Incorrect	Correct
josle	**jostle**	jungel	**jungle**
joting	**jotting**	junkture	**juncture**
joveal	**jovial**	jurie	**jury**
joyus	**joyous**	jurk	**jerk**
jubalee	**jubilee**	jurnal	**journal**
judishary	**judiciary**	justefy	**justify**
juge	**judge**	justise	**justice**
jugler	**juggler**	juvinile	**juvenile**

Look-Alikes or Sound-Alikes

jam *to squeeze; a sweet spread* • **jamb** *side of door*

jealous *envious* • **zealous** *enthusiastic*

jeer *to scoff* • **cheer** *to applaud*

jester *clown* • **gesture** *movement*

Jewry *Jews* • **jury** *court*

Jews *Semitic* • **chews** *eats* • **choose** *select*

jibe *gibe* • **gibe** *to sneer at* • **gybe** *in sailing, to swing from side to side*

jinks *lively frolics* • **jinx** *bad luck*

joust *to join battle* • **just** *equitable*

juggler *one who juggles* • **jugular** *throat*

just *equitable* • **joust** *to join battle*

k

Incorrect	Correct
kadet	**cadet**
kaff	**calf**
kahki	**khaki**
kameleon	**chameleon**
kangeroo	**kangaroo**
kanoo	**canoe**
kaos	**chaos**
kapput	**kaput**
karacter	**character**
karof	**carafe**
kash	**cash**
kasm	**chasm**
katar	**catarrh**
kaynine	**canine**
kazm	**chasm**
keal	**keel**
kean	**keen**
kee	**key**
Keltic	**Celtic**
ken	**can**
kenel	**kennel**
keoty	**coyote**
kep	**kept**
kerasene	**kerosene**
kernel	**colonel**
kerst	**cursed**
kertin	**curtain**
kerupt	**corrupt**
kerve	**curve**
ketch	**catch**
ketel	**kettle**
kiak	**kayak**
kichin	**kitchen**
kidnee	**kidney**
kik	**kick**
kiler	**killer**
killowatt	**kilowatt**
kimona	**kimono**
kindel	**kindle**
kindergarden	**kindergarten**
kindrid	**kindred**
kiness	**kindness**
kingdum	**kingdom**
kiper	**kipper**
kiropedy	**chiropody**
kist	**kissed**
kitastrofy	**catastrophe**
kitin	**kitten**
kiyoty	**coyote**
klak	**claque**
kleek	**clique**
klorine	**chlorine**
knifes	**knives**
knoted	**knotted**
knowlege	**knowledge**
kolic	**colic**
kolyumnist	**columnist**

Incorrect	Correct	Incorrect	Correct
komfortable	**comfortable**	Kremlen	**Kremlin**
koming	**coming**	kriptic	**cryptic**
kommunist	**communist**	kronic	**chronic**
koral	**choral**	kugele	**cudgel**
koris	**chorus**	kwik	**quick**
korz	**corps**	kwire	**choir**
kraft	**craft**	kwire	**quire**

Look-Alikes or Sound-Alikes

kerb *edge of pavement* • **curb** *to check*

kernel *seed* • **colonel** *officer*

key *with lock* • **quay** *dock*

kill *murder* • **kiln** *oven*

knave *fool* • **nave** *part of church*

knead *to press* • **need** *must have*

kneel *to rest on the knees* • **Neil** *man's name*

knew *did know* • **gnu** *animal* • **new** *not old*

knight *feudal rank* • **night** *opposite of day*

knit *form fabric* • **nit** *insect*

knock *to strike* • **nock** *notch of an arrow*

knot *what you tie* • **not** *no*

know *to understand* • **no** *opposite of yes*

knows *understands* • **noes** *negatives* • **nose** *on face*

kohl *eye shadow* • **coal** *fire* • **koel** *a cuckoo*

kola *a nut or tree* • **cola** *a drink*

kris *cheese; dagger* • **crease** *fold*

l

Incorrect	Correct
labedo	**libido**
laber	**labour**
labidinus	**libidinous**
labirinth	**labyrinth**
lable	**label**
labratory	**laboratory**
laceing	**lacing**
lasserate	**lacerate**
lach	**latch**
laciny	**larceny**
lacker	**lacquer**
lacksitive	**laxative**
ladel	**ladle**
lader	**ladder**
ladys	**ladies**
laffable	**laughable**
laffter	**laughter**
lagard	**laggard**
lage	**large**
laging	**lagging**
laik	**lake**
laim	**lame**
laison	**liaison**
lait	**late**
lakey	**lackey**
lakrimos	**lachrymose**
lakwashus	**loquacious**
lamanate	**laminate**
lamentible	**lamentable**
lanalin	**lanolin**
langer	**languor**
langwidge	**language**
langwish	**languish**
lanlord	**landlord**
lanscape	**landscape**
lanse	**lance**
lantin	**lantern**
lanzheree	**lingerie**
lapell	**lapel**
larinx	**larynx**
lasatude	**lassitude**
lase	**lace**
laserate	**lacerate**
lasie	**lassie**
lasivious	**lascivious**
laso	**lasso**
latatude	**latitude**
laticework	**latticework**
latly	**lately**
lattent	**latent**
laughible	**laughable**
laveleer	**lavaliere**
lavinda	**lavender**
lavitory	**lavatory**
Lawd	**Lord**
lawdible	**laudable**
lawndry	**laundry**
layed	**laid**

ncorrect	Correct
aywer	**lawyer**
azyness	**laziness**
eafs	**leaves**
eakige	**leakage**
eanyent	**lenient**
easure	**leisure**
eathil	**lethal**
eazon	**liaison**
ecksacon	**lexicon**
econic	**laconic**
edgislature	**legislature**
eeder	**leader**
eeg	**league**
eese	**lease**
eftenant	**lieutenant**
egallize	**legalize**
eger	**ledger**
egil	**legal**
eging	**legging**
egitamate	**legitimate**
Leibfraumilch	**Liebfraumilch**
eif	**leaf**
eige	**liege**
eisurly	**leisurely**
ejable	**legible**
ejend	**legend**
lejerdeman	**legerdemain**
lejon	**legion**
ekcher	**lecture**
lemenade	**lemonade**
ended	**lent**

Incorrect	Correct
lenth	**length**
lenz	**lens**
leperd	**leopard**
lepersy	**leprosy**
leprakon	**leprechaun**
lept	**leapt**
lern	**learn**
lesen	**lesson**
less	**let's**
leter	**letter**
lether	**leather**
lethergy	**lethargy**
letice	**lettuce**
letterd	**lettered**
lettup	**letup**
levatation	**levitation**
leve	**leave**
leven	**eleven**
leven	**leaven**
levle	**level**
levler	**leveller**
lew	**lieu**
lezbian	**lesbian**
liberalizm	**liberalism**
liberry	**library**
libility	**liability**
lible	**libel**
libral	**liberal**
libreto	**libretto**
licker	**liquor**
lickrish	**licorice**
lieing	**lying**

Incorrect	Correct
liem	**lime**
lier	**liar**
lifboat	**lifeboat**
lifes	**lives**
liftime	**lifetime**
ligiment	**ligament**
likker	**liquor**
likly	**likely**
likness	**likeness**
lillac	**lilac**
lilly	**lily**
lim	**limb**
limazine	**limousine**
limba	**limber**
limf	**lymph**
limlite	**limelight**
limmit	**limit**
lingwist	**linguist**
linier	**linear**
linkige	**linkage**
linnen	**linen**
linnoleum	**linoleum**
linx	**lynx**
liqued	**liquid**
liquify	**liquefy**
liric	**lyric**
lisenshus	**licentious**
lisome	**lissome**
lissen	**listen**
lite	**light**
litergical	**liturgical**
litracy	**literacy**

Incorrect	Correct
litrature	**literature**
littany	**litany**
littul	**little**
liven	**enliven**
livelyhood	**livelihood**
livlihood	**livelihood**
livly	**lively**
livry	**livery**
lizzard	**lizard**
lobey	**lobby**
lobrow	**lowbrow**
locallize	**localize**
locamotive	**locomotive**
lockket	**locket**
lofer	**loafer**
logarhythm	**logarithm**
logerithm	**logarithm**
loggic	**logic**
loial	**loyal**
loje	**lodge**
lokist	**locust**
lokspur	**larkspur**
lon	**lawn**
lonch	**launch**
lonjevaty	**longevity**
lonjitude	**longitude**
lonliness	**loneliness**
lonly	**lonely**
lonsome	**lonesome**
lood	**lewd**
loonatic	**lunatic**
loor	**lure**

Incorrect	Correct
loosid	**lucid**
loover	**louvre**
Loovre	**Louvre**
looze	**lose**
lor	**lore**
Loraly	**Lorelei**
lorel	**laurel**
lornyet	**lorgnette**
los	**loss**
loshun	**lotion**
lotery	**lottery**
lothe	**loathe**
loveable	**lovable**
loveing	**loving**
lovly	**lovely**
lowd	**loud**
lownje	**lounge**
lowt	**lout**
lubercate	**lubricate**
ludacrus	**ludicrous**
luet	**lute**
lugage	**luggage**
luke	**luck**
lukshurient	**luxuriant**
lukwarm	**lukewarm**
lulaby	**lullaby**
luminecent	**luminescent**
lunasy	**lunacy**
lushous	**luscious**
lusterous	**lustrous**
luv	**love**
luxry	**luxury**
lyeing	**lying**
lyon	**lion**

Look-Alikes or Sound-Alikes

lain *did lie on* • **lane** *path*

lair *den* • **layer** *a thickness; fold*

lam *run away* • **lamb** *young sheep*

laser *a beam of coherent light* • **lazar** *a leper*

later *afterwards* • **latter** *the last one of two*

lath *strip of wood* • **lathe** *a machine tool*

laud *praise* • **lord** *noble*

lava *of volcano* • **larva** *of insect*

lay *to deposit* • **lei** *wreath*

lazar *a leper* • **laser** *beam of coherent light*

lead *metal; to guide* • **led** *did guide*

leaf *tree* • **lief** *gladly*

leak *crack* • **leek** *vegetable*

lean *thin* • **lien** *legal charge*

least *smallest* • **lest** *unless*

lessee *tenant* • **lesser** *smaller* • **lessor** *one who leases*

lessen *to decrease* • **lesson** *instruction*

levee *dike* • **levy** *fine, tax*

liable *obligated* • **libel** *slander*

liar *tells lies* • **lyre** *musical instrument*

licence *the noun* • **license** *the verb*

licorice *a flavouring* • **lickerish** *eager, craving*

lie *falsehood* • **lye** *chemical*

lief *gladly* • **leaf** *tree*

lien *legal charge* • **lean** *thin*

lightening *making lighter, relieving* • **lightning** *flash in sky*

linage *number of lines* • **lineage** *ancestry*

lineament *one of the contours of the body* • **liniment** *a thin ointment*

links *joins* • **lynx** *animal*

liqueur *sweet liquor* • **liquor** *alcoholic drink*

lo! *exclamation* • **low** *down; base*

load *burden* • **lode** *mineral*

loan *lending* • **lone** *alone*

loath *reluctant* • **loathe** *despise*

local *not widespread* • **locale** *a locality*

loch *lake* • **lock** *fastening*

ocks *fastenings* • **lox** *almon*

ocus *a place; locality* • **ocust** *insect*

oose *not tight* • **lose** *fail to vin; mislay*

oot *booty* • **lute** *musical nstrument*

ord *noble* • **laud** *praise*

lumbar *part of body* • **lumber** *wood* • *to move clumsily*

luxuriance *state of being luxurious* • **luxuriant** *exceedingly fertile* • **luxurious** *sumptuous*

lye *chemical* • **lie** *falsehood*

lynx *animal* • **links** *joins*

m

Incorrect	Correct
macarune	**macaroon**
maccadim	**macadam**
maccaroni	**macaroni**
machurashun	**maturation**
machure	**mature**
macintosh	**mackintosh**
mackrel	**mackerel**
madalion	**medallion**
maddame	**madam**
madmwazel	**mademoiselle**
madres	**madras**
magizine	**magazine**
magnatude	**magnitude**
magnifasense	**magnificence**
magnit	**magnet**
magot	**maggot**
magnut	**magnet**
mahiraja	**maharajah**
maibe	**maybe**
maidnly	**maidenly**
mainger	**manger**
mainia	**mania**
maintainance	**maintenance**
maionaize	**mayonnaise**
maitriarc	**matriarch**
majer	**major**
majik	**magic**
majistrat	**magistrate**
majoraty	**majority**
Makavelian	**Machiavellian**
makeing	**making**
maladikshun	**malediction**
malase	**malice**
malfezence	**malfeasance**
maliable	**malleable**
maline	**malign**
malingger	**malinger**
malishus	**malicious**
mallady	**malady**
mallis	**malice**
mamal	**mammal**
mamalade	**marmalade**
mamuth	**mammoth**
manacure	**manicure**
manafacture	**manufacture**
manafesto	**manifesto**
manafold	**manifold**
managable	**manageable**
manajer	**manager**
manditory	**mandatory**
maner	**manner**
manicle	**manacle**
manje	**mange**
manjer	**manger**
manogamist	**monogamist**

Incorrect	Correct
manotinus	**monotonous**
manshun	**mansion**
mantlpeace	**mantelpiece**
manuscrip	**manuscript**
manur	**manure**
manuver	**manoeuvre**
mapul	**maple**
maraskino	**maraschino**
maratime	**maritime**
marawana	**marijuana**
marbel	**marble**
mareen	**marine**
marige	**marriage**
marjerin	**margarine**
marjin	**margin**
markee	**marquee**
markez	**marquise**
markit	**market**
marod	**maraud**
marow	**marrow**
marriagable	**marriageable**
marrie	**marry**
marryed	**married**
marteeni	**martini**
marter	**martyr**
marune	**maroon**
marvilus	**marvellous**
masaje	**massage**
masaker	**massacre**
mascuelin	**masculine**
mashety	**machete**
mashinery	**machinery**
Masichusetts	**Massachusetts**
masinry	**masonry**
masive	**massive**
maskerade	**masquerade**
masta	**master**
mastacate	**masticate**
masur	**masseur**
mater	**matter**
mater de	**maître d'**
maternaty	**maternity**
mathamatics	**mathematics**
matinay	**matinée**
matramony	**matrimony**
matrinly	**matronly**
matris	**mattress**
matterial	**material**
mavrick	**maverick**
mawl	**maul**
maxamum	**maximum**
maylanje	**mélange**
mazoleum	**mausoleum**
meaness	**meanness**
meanyal	**menial**
mecanic	**mechanic**
medamorfisis	**metamorphosis**
medecine	**medicine**
medeocker	**mediocre**
Mediteranean	**Mediterranean**
medl	**medal**

Incorrect	Correct	Incorrect	Correct
medle	**meddle**	merderer	**murderer**
medly	**medley**	merdger	**merger**
medow	**meadow**	meret	**merit**
meedjum	**medium**	merly	**merely**
meeger	**meagre**	mermer	**murmur**
meeteor	**meteor**	merryly	**merrily**
meglomania	**megalomania**	mersy	**mercy**
mein	**mien**	mesenger	**messenger**
mekanize	**mechanize**	mesure	**measure**
melincoly	**melancholy**	mesy	**messy**
mellodrama	**melodrama**	mesyur	**monsieur**
mellodious	**melodious**	metafor	**metaphor**
mellon	**melon**	meterial	**material**
melow	**mellow**	Methadist	**Methodist**
memberane	**membrane**	metripolitan	**metropolitan**
memmento	**memento**	mettalic	**metallic**
memmorial	**memorial**	metul	**metal**
memrable	**memorable**	meucus	**mucous**
memry	**memory**	mezaneen	**mezzanine**
memwar	**memoir**	mezels	**measles**
menajery	**menagerie**	mezmerize	**mesmerize**
menise	**menace**	micrascope	**microscope**
menshun	**mention**	miday	**midday**
ment	**meant**	middel	**middle**
menstrate	**menstruate**	midevil	**medieval**
mentle	**mental**	miksture	**mixture**
meny	**many**	milage	**mileage**
menyu	**menu**	milatery	**military**
merang	**meringue**	milenium	**millennium**
merchindize	**merchandise**	milinary	**millinery**
mercinery	**mercenary**	milionaire	**millionaire**
merderer	**mercenary**	millicha	**militia**

Incorrect	Correct
milldew	**mildew**
minamum	**minimum**
minature	**miniature**
mingel	**mingle**
miniral	**mineral**
minis	**minus**
miniscule	**minuscule**
ministor	**minister**
minit	**minute**
minnimum	**minimum**
minoraty	**minority**
minse	**mince**
minusha	**minutiae**
miopia	**myopia**
miricle	**miracle**
miror	**mirror**
mirraje	**mirage**
mirtle	**myrtle**
mischevous	**mischievous**
mischif	**mischief**
mise	**mice**
miselaneous	**miscellaneous**
mishin	**mission**
Misissippi	**Mississippi**
mislayed	**mislaid**
mispell	**misspell**
misquito	**mosquito**
misrable	**miserable**
misry	**misery**
missconduct	**misconduct**
misseltoe	**mistletoe**
missfortune	**misfortune**
misshap	**mishap**
missojiny	**misogyny**
misstake	**mistake**
mistacizm	**mysticism**
mistakeable	**mistakable**
mistate	**misstate**
misterious	**mysterious**
mistery	**mystery**
mistify	**mystify**
mistris	**mistress**
mithical	**mythical**
mittin	**mitten**
mizer	**miser**
mizerable	**miserable**
moap	**mope**
mobillize	**mobilize**
mocassin	**moccasin**
modifyer	**modifier**
modil	**model**
modist	**modest**
modren	**modern**
Mohamedin	**Muhammadan**
mohoginy	**mahogany**
mojulate	**modulate**
mokery	**mockery**
molatto	**mulatto**
molify	**mollify**
mollecule	**molecule**
mollestation	**molestation**
mommentus	**momentous**

Incorrect	Correct	Incorrect	Correct
monark	**monarch**	moteef	**motif**
mone	**moan**	moter	**motor**
monistery	**monastery**	motled	**mottled**
monitone	**monotone**	movment	**movement**
monopolly	**monopoly**	moyschur	**moisture**
monsterous	**monstrous**	mozaic	**mosaic**
mony	**money**	mudy	**muddy**
moraleity	**morality**	muleish	**mulish**
moray	**moiré**	multaply	**multiply**
mordlin	**maudlin**	mundain	**mundane**
Moreman	**Mormon**	munkey	**monkey**
morfeen	**morphine**	munth	**month**
morg	**morgue**	murmer	**murmur**
morgage	**mortgage**	murr	**myrrh**
mornfull	**mournful**	musell	**muscle**
Moroco	**Morocco**	musilije	**mucilage**
morsal	**morsel**	mustache	**moustache**
mortafy	**mortify**	mustid	**mustard**
mortaly	**mortally**	mutny	**mutiny**
mortuery	**mortuary**	muzeem	**museum**
moshin	**motion**	muzik	**music**
mosk	**mosque**	muzlin	**muslin**
mosy	**mossy**	myazma	**miasma**
mote	**moat**	mygrate	**migrate**

Look-Alikes or Sound-Alikes

made *did make* • **maid** *servant*

magna *great* • **magma** *rock*

magnate *prominent person* • **magnet** *attracts iron*

mail *letters* • **male** *man*

main *principal* • **mane** *hair of animal*

maize *corn* • **maze** *confusing paths*

manner *method* • **manor** *estate*

mantel *shelf at fireplace* • **mantle** *cloak*

marc *refuse remaining after pressing seeds, fruits* • **mark** *sign*

marital *in marriage* • **marshal** *official* • **martial** *warlike*

mark *sign* • **marc** *refuse remaining after pressing seeds, fruits*

marriage *wedding* • **mirage** *illusion*

marry *wed* • **merry** *jolly* • **Mary** *girl's name*

mascle *a steel plate* • **muscle** *tissue of the body* • **mussel** *shellfish*

mask *cover* • **masque** *masked ball*

mason *bricklayer* • **meson** *in physics, a particle*

maybe *perhaps* • **may be** *may happen*

mayor *town* • **mare** *female horse*

maze *confusing paths* • **maize** *corn*

mean *nasty* • **mien** *bearing*

meat *food* • **meet** *encounter* • **mete** *apportion*

medal *award* • **meddle** *interfere* • **mettle** *spirit* • **metal** *material*

meet *encounter* • **meat** *food* • **mete** *apportion*

merry *jolly* • **Mary** *girl's name* • **marry** *wed*

meson *in physics, a particle* • **mason** *a bricklayer*

meteorology *study of atmosphere* • **metrology** *system of weights and measures*

mendacity *lying* • **mendicity** *begging*

meter *measuring device for gas etc.* • **metre** *for poetry; unit of length*

mews *cat's sounds; row of stables* • **muse** *think*

might *strength; may* • **mite** *small insect; small child*

mil *unit of measure* • **mill** *grinding machine; factory*

militate *contend, tell (against)* • **mitigate** *to ease*

millenary *a thousand years* • **millinery** *hats*

millinery *hats* • **millinary** *a thousand years*

mince *to cut into small pieces* • **mints** *places where money is made; sweets*

mind *brain; object to; care for* • **mined** *dug*

miner *one who mines* • **minor** *below legal age; unimportant*

Minister *government* • **minister** *aid* • **minster** *cathedral*

mints *places where money is made; sweets* • **mince** *to cut into small pieces*

mirage *illusion* • **marriage** *wedding*

Miss *single woman* • **Mrs** *married woman* • **Ms** *substitute for Mrs or Miss* • **mss.** *manuscripts*

missal *book for Mass* • **missile** *weapon*

missed *failed* • **mist** *haze*

moat *ditch* • **mote** *small particle*

mode *manner* • **mowed** *cut down*

moral *lesson* • **morale** *spirit*

morn *morning* • **mourn** *grieve*

morning *a.m.* • **mourning** *grieving*

mote *small particle* • **moat** *ditch*

motif *theme* • **motive** *reason*

mudder *a horse* • **mother** *a female parent*

muscle *tissue of the body* • **mussel** *shellfish* • **mascle** *a steel plate*

muse *think* • **mews** *cat's sounds; row of stables*

mussel *shellfish* • **muscle** *tissue of the body* • **mascle** *a steel plate*

Muslim *religion* • **muslin** *cloth*

mustard *spice* • **mustered** *summoned*

n

Incorrect	Correct
nabor	**neighbour**
nachurally	**naturally**
nack	**knack**
nacotics	**narcotics**
nafairius	**nefarious**
naftha	**naphtha**
naged	**nagged**
naivtay	**naïveté**
nale	**nail**
namless	**nameless**
namonia	**pneumonia**
napsack	**knapsack**
naration	**narration**
narative	**narrative**
narl	**gnarl**
narow	**narrow**
narsistic	**narcissistic**
narwhale	**narwhal**
nasent	**nascent**
nash	**gnash**
nashunel	**national**
nastershum	**nasturtium**
nastyness	**nastiness**
nat	**gnat**
natchur	**nature**
nausha	**nausea**
navagable	**navigable**
navey	**navy**
naw	**gnaw**
naybor	**neighbour**
nazal	**nasal**
nebulus	**nebulous**
necesery	**necessary**
necesity	**necessity**
neckromansy	**necromancy**
nectereen	**nectarine**
nee	**knee**
needel	**needle**
neet	**neat**
neether	**neither**
nefew	**nephew**
negitive	**negative**
neglajence	**negligence**
negleck	**neglect**
neglejay	**negligée**
negligeable	**negligible**
negoshiate	**negotiate**
neice	**niece**
nek	**neck**
nekachif	**neckerchief**
nekkid	**naked**
neks	**next**
nemonic	**mnemonic**
neppotizm	**nepotism**
nere	**near**
nerse	**nurse**
nerviss	**nervous**
nesecery	**necessary**

Incorrect	Correct
nesessity	**necessity**
nesle	**nestle**
neumatic	**pneumatic**
neumonia	**pneumonia**
newsance	**nuisance**
Niagra	**Niagara**
nializm	**nihilism**
nible	**nibble**
nicateen	**nicotine**
nich	**niche**
nickle	**nickel**
nicknack	**knick-knack**
nicly	**nicely**
nieve	**naïve**
nife	**knife**
nill	**nil**
nimbel	**nimble**
nimf	**nymph**
ninedy	**ninety**
nineth	**ninth**
ninteen	**nineteen**
ninty	**ninety**
nippal	**nipple**
nite	**night**
nob	**knob**
nobles oblege	**noblesse oblige**
noblman	**nobleman**
nocean	**notion**
noch	**notch**
nock	**knock**
nockternil	**nocturnal**

Incorrect	Correct
nohow	**know-how**
noisesome	**noisome**
nokshus	**noxious**
noll	**knoll**
nollage	**knowledge**
nome	**gnome**
nomminate	**nominate**
nonnentity	**nonentity**
nonshalant	**nonchalant**
noo	**new**
nooclear	**nuclear**
nooratic	**neurotic**
noosance	**nuisance**
noot	**knout**
nootral	**neutral**
noovo reesh	**nouveau riche**
normel	**normal**
northernly	**northerly**
notery	**notary**
noth	**north**
notible	**notable**
noticable	**noticeable**
notise	**notice**
nottorious	**notorious**
noval	**novel**
novis	**novice**
no where	**nowhere**
nowledge	**knowledge**
noyz	**noise**
nozgay	**nosegay**
nu	**new**

Incorrect	Correct	Incorrect	Correct
nuckle	**knuckle**	nurologist	**neurologist**
nucleous	**nucleus**	nurserys	**nurseries**
nudaty	**nudity**	nursmaid	**nursemaid**
nuklear	**nuclear**	nusence	**nuisance**
nulification	**nullification**	nustaljic	**nostalgic**
num	**numb**	nuthing	**nothing**
numbskull	**numskull**	nutralise	**neutralize**
numrous	**numerous**	nutrishon	**nutrition**
nunery	**nunnery**	nuty	**nutty**
nupshal	**nuptial**	nyeev	**naïve**
nuralja	**neuralgia**	nyether	**neither**
nurish	**nourish**	nyew	**new**

Look-Alikes or Sound-Alikes

naval *navy* • **navel** *stomach*

nave *part of church* • **knave** *fool*

nay *no* • **neigh** *horse's sound*

need *lack* • **knead** *to press*

Neil *man's name* • **kneel** *to rest on the knees*

new *not old* • **knew** *did know* • **gnu** *animal*

night *opposite of day* • **knight** *feudal rank*

nit *insect* • **knit** *form fabric*

no *opposite of yes* • **know** *to understand*

nob *head* • **knob** *handle*

noble *aristocratic* • **Nobel** *the prize*

nocturn *a midnight prayer* • **nocturne** *musical piece*

noes *negatives* • **nose** *on face* • **knows** *understands*

none *not one* • **nun** *religious*

not *no* • **knot** *what you tie*

O

Incorrect	Correct
obay	**obey**
obcelete	**obsolete**
obedeance	**obedience**
obees	**obese**
obichuary	**obituary**
obitrator	**arbitrator**
objeck	**object**
objeckshunable	**objectionable**
obleck	**oblique**
oblidge	**oblige**
obligatto	**obbligato**
obnocshus	**obnoxious**
obseekweus	**obsequious**
obseen	**obscene**
obseshun	**obsession**
obsolecent	**obsolescent**
obstratrishin	**obstetrician**
obstickal	**obstacle**
obstonite	**obstinate**
obvius	**obvious**
obzervance	**observance**
ocasion	**occasion**
occassionel	**occasional**
occer	**occur**
occulist	**oculist**
occupent	**occupant**
occupyed	**occupied**
occurance	**occurrence**
octapus	**octopus**
ocupancy	**occupancy**
ocurr	**occur**
od	**odd**
Oddisy	**Odyssey**
oder	**odour**
oderus	**odorous**
ofen	**often**
ofer	**offer**
offense	**offence**
offring	**offering**
ofice	**office**
oficial	**official**
ofishus	**officious**
ofthamology	**ophthalmology**
oger	**ogre**
ogil	**ogle**
oister	**oyster**
ole	**old**
olfaktry	**olfactory**
Olimpic	**Olympic**
ollive	**olive**
omishin	**omission**
omisible	**omissible**
omlet	**omelette**
omminous	**ominous**
ommitt	**omit**
omnishent	**omniscient**

Incorrect	Correct
omniverus	**omnivorous**
onarus	**onerous**
oncore	**encore**
onest	**honest**
on mass	**en masse**
onor	**honour**
onorable	**honourable**
onorary	**honorary**
onroot	**en route**
onsomble	**ensemble**
ontorage	**entourage**
ontraprenor	**entrepreneur**
ontray	**entrée**
onvelope	**envelope**
opaik	**opaque**
openess	**openness**
opin	**open**
opinyun	**opinion**
opis	**opus**
oponent	**opponent**
oportune	**opportune**
oportunity	**opportunity**
opose	**oppose**
opperator	**operator**
oppeum	**opium**
opponant	**opponent**
opra	**opera**
oprate	**operate**
opresser	**oppressor**
opreta	**operetta**
opry	**opera**
opshinul	**optional**
optishin	**optician**
optomism	**optimism**
oragin	**origin**
orbut	**orbit**
orchester	**orchestra**
ordinence	**ordinance**
ordinry	**ordinary**
ore	**oar**
orevoir	**au revoir**
orfan	**orphan**
orful	**awful**
orgazm	**orgasm**
orgin	**organ**
orgment	**augment**
oricul	**oracle**
orignal	**original**
oringe	**orange**
orjy	**orgy**
orkid	**orchid**
orniment	**ornament**
orrator	**orator**
ors d'oeurves	**hors d'oeuvres**
orstritch	**ostrich**
orthentik	**authentic**
ortherdox	**orthodox**
orthorety	**authority**
orthorize	**authorize**
oscullatory	**osculatory**
oshan	**ocean**
osheanografi	**oceanography**

Incorrect	Correct	Incorrect	Correct
osify	**ossify**	overeach	**overreach**
osillate	**oscillate**	overought	**overwrought**
osstensible	**ostensible**	overser	**overseer**
ostintashus	**ostentatious**	overun	**overrun**
othe	**oath**	overwelm	**overwhelm**
our's	**ours**	overy	**ovary**
ourselfs	**ourselves**	ovurt	**overt**
outragous	**outrageous**	ownce	**ounce**
outsidder	**outsider**	owst	**oust**
outter	**outer**	oxagen	**oxygen**
outwerd	**outward**	oxes	**oxen**
ovature	**overture**	oyl	**oil**
overate	**overrate**	oyntment	**ointment**

Look-Alikes or Sound-Alikes

oar *boat* • **o'er** *over* • **or** *alternative* • **ore** *mineral* • **awe** *fear*

ode *poem* • **owed** *did owe*

of *belonging to* • **off** *away from*

older *refers to age only* • **elder** *refers to age and wisdom gained*

one *single* • **won** *did win*

opposite *other side* • **apposite** *suitable*

oral *verbal* • **aural** *hearing*

ordinance *law* • **ordnance** *military supply*

oscillate *vibrate* • **osculate** *kiss*

ought *should* • **aught** *anything*

our *belongs to us* • **hour** *time*

owed *did owe* • **ode** *poem*

p

Incorrect	Correct
packige	**package**
Packistan	**Pakistan**
padestrian	**pedestrian**
padjamas	**pyjamas**
padray	**padre**
pagent	**pageant**
pakage	**package**
pakt	**pact**
pallace	**palace**
pallacial	**palatial**
pallasade	**palisade**
pallatable	**palatable**
pallit	**palate**
pallour	**pallor**
pallsey	**palsy**
palpatate	**palpitate**
palpible	**palpable**
pam	**palm**
pamistry	**palmistry**
pamphalet	**pamphlet**
pandamoneum	**pandemonium**
pandcake	**pancake**
panerama	**panorama**
panicea	**panacea**
panicy	**panicky**
panitela	**panatella**
pannel	**panel**
pantamime	**pantomime**
panyless	**penniless**
panzy	**pansy**
paper-mashe	**papier-mâché**
papisy	**papacy**
pappriker	**paprika**
parafrase	**paraphrase**
paralise	**paralyse**
parcly	**parsley**
pardner	**partner**
parfay	**parfait**
paridice	**paradise**
parifernalia	**paraphernalia**
parisite	**parasite**
parkay	**parquet**
parlement	**parliament**
parler	**parlour**
Parmizan (cheese)	**Parmesan**
parodocks	**paradox**
parot	**parrot**
parraboler	**parabola**
parrade	**parade**
parrafin	**paraffin**
parragraf	**paragraph**
parralel	**parallel**
parralisis	**paralysis**
parramount	**paramount**

Incorrect	Correct	Incorrect	Correct
parratrooper	**paratrooper**	pasive	**passive**
parrenthasis	**parenthesis**	paso	**peso**
parrible	**parable**	pasport	**passport**
parridy	**parody**	passifist	**pacifist**
parrikeet	**parakeet**	passta	**pasta**
parrish	**parish**	passtell	**pastel**
parrishute	**parachute**	passtime	**pastime**
parrity	**parity**	passtrami	**pastrami**
parrocheal	**parochial**	pastachio	**pistachio**
parrole	**parole**	pasteing	**pasting**
parrson	**parson**	paster	**pastor**
parrymecium	**paramecium**	pastrey	**pastry**
parry-mutual	**pari-mutuel**	pasturize	**pasteurize**
parsel	**parcel**	patata	**potato**
parshel	**partial**	patern	**pattern**
partasiple	**participle**	paticular	**particular**
partative	**partitive**	patition	**petition**
partickle	**particle**	patritism	**patriotism**
partickuler	**particular**	patriyot	**patriot**
partishun	**partition**	patroleum	**petroleum**
partisipate	**participate**	pattedifoigra	**pâté de foie gras**
partizan	**partisan**	pattent	**patent**
partys	**parties**	patternal	**paternal**
parynoia	**paranoia**	pattio	**patio**
parypledgic	**paraplegic**	patren	**patron**
pasay	**passé**	pattrol	**patrol**
pashent	**patient**	paveing	**paving**
pashion	**passion**	pavilon	**pavilion**
pasible	**passable**	pavment	**pavement**
pasidge	**passage**	pawlbarer	**pallbearer**
Pasific	**Pacific**	payed	**paid**
pasify	**pacify**		

Incorrect	Correct
paysley	**paisley**
payso	**peso**
paythos	**pathos**
pean	**paean**
peavish	**peevish**
pecunerary	**pecuniary**
pedagree	**pedigree**
pedistal	**pedestal**
peeanist	**pianist**
peech	**peach**
peedyatrics	**pediatrics**
peenil	**penal**
peenut	**peanut**
peepul	**people**
pees	**peas**
peeza	**pizza**
pegoda	**pagoda**
peice	**piece**
peirce	**pierce**
pekan	**pecan**
pelet	**pellet**
pellmell	**pell-mell**
pemanship	**penmanship**
penant	**pennant**
penatenshary	**penitentiary**
penatint	**penitent**
penatrate	**penetrate**
penelty	**penalty**
penife	**penknife**
penndyalum	**pendulum**
pennicilan	**penicillin**
penninsuler	**peninsula**
penntegon	**pentagon**
penoir	**peignoir**
pensil	**pencil**
Pentacostal	**Pentecostal**
peraps	**perhaps**
percalator	**percolator**
percarious	**precarious**
percaution	**precaution**
percept	**precept**
percieve	**perceive**
percise	**precise**
perclude	**preclude**
perculiar	**peculiar**
percushion	**percussion**
perdict	**predict**
perdikament	**predicament**
perdominant	**predominant**
perel	**peril**
perfer	**prefer**
perferate	**perforate**
perfessor	**professor**
perfict	**perfect**
perge	**purge**
perliminary	**preliminary**
permenant	**permanent**
permiate	**permeate**
permisable	**permissible**
permitt	**permit**
permonition	**premonition**
perpare	**prepare**
perpatrate	**perpetrate**

Incorrect	Correct	Incorrect	Correct
perpettual	**perpetual**	persuit	**pursuit**
perpindicular	**perpendicular**	persumption	**presumption**
perple	**purple**	perswade	**persuade**
perponderant	**preponderant**	pertanint	**pertinent**
perport	**purport**	pertato	**potato**
perposterous	**preposterous**	pertend	**pretend**
perpulsion	**propulsion**	perticulars	**particulars**
perranum	**per annum**	pertition	**petition**
perrascope	**periscope**	pervail	**prevail**
perrenial	**perennial**	pervention	**prevention**
perrifery	**periphery**	pervide	**provide**
perrimter	**perimeter**	pesimist	**pessimist**
perriod	**period**	pestaside	**pesticide**
perroxide	**peroxide**	petteet	**petite**
persavere	**persevere**	pettle	**petal**
perscribe	**prescribe**	pettrify	**petrify**
perscription	**prescription**	pettulant	**petulant**
perse	**purse**	pettycoat	**petticoat**
persent	**per cent**	peverse	**perverse**
persepectus	**prospectus**	pezint	**peasant**
perser	**purser**	Pharow	**Pharaoh**
perserve	**preserve**	phasician	**physician**
persikute	**persecute**	phaze	**phase**
persin	**person**	pheenix	**phoenix**
persistance	**persistence**	pheenobarbatal	**phenobarbital**
personnal	**personal**	philip	**fillip**
perspacacous	**perspicacious**	Philipino	**Filipino**
persue	**pursue**	phillately	**philately**
		Phillidelphia	**Philadelphia**
		Phillipines	**Philippines**
		phinomenon	**phenomenon**

Incorrect	Correct
phisics	**physics**
phisionomy	**physiognomy**
phisique	**physique**
phisyology	**physiology**
phisyotherapy	**physiotherapy**
phonettic	**phonetic**
phonnics	**phonics**
phosferous	**phosphorus**
phosforresence	**phosphorescence**
photagraph	**photograph**
phylanthropy	**philanthropy**
physiclly	**physically**
piana	**piano**
piaza	**piazza**
picadilo	**peccadillo**
piccyune	**picayune**
pich	**pitch**
pickel	**pickle**
picknic	**picnic**
picollo	**piccolo**
pidgeon	**pigeon**
pietty	**piety**
piggment	**pigment**
pika	**pica**
piket	**picket**
pilage	**pillage**
pilbox	**pillbox**
pileing	**piling**
pilet	**pilot**
pilgrum	**pilgrim**
piller	**pillar**
pillery	**pillory**
pillfer	**pilfer**
pillgrum	**pilgrim**
pimmento	**pimento**
pimpel	**pimple**
pinacle	**pinnacle**
pinapple	**pineapple**
pinnup	**pinup**
pinsers	**pincers**
pinurious	**penurious**
pionner	**pioneer**
pipeing	**piping**
piramid	**pyramid**
pire	**pyre**
pirex	**Pyrex**
piromaniac	**pyromaniac**
pirotechnics	**pyrotechnics**
pistin	**piston**
pitchur	**picture**
pitence	**pittance**
pittfall	**pitfall**
Pittsburg	**Pittsburgh**
pittuitary	**pituitary**
pitty	**pity**
pityful	**pitiful**
pivit	**pivot**
placcate	**placate**
plackard	**placard**
placment	**placement**
plad	**plaid**

Incorrect	Correct	Incorrect	Correct
plage	**plague**	pluss	**plus**
plajiarism	**plagiarism**	pluttonium	**plutonium**
plannet	**planet**	plyable	**pliable**
plannetarium	**planetarium**	plyers	**pliers**
plasa	**plaza**	pocession	**possession**
plasebo	**placebo**	pockabook	**pocketbook**
plassid	**placid**	pockit	**pocket**
plasstic	**plastic**	poggrom	**pogrom**
platow	**plateau**	poinyant	**poignant**
plater	**platter**	poisin	**poison**
plattform	**platform**	poit	**poet**
plattinum	**platinum**	poize	**poise**
plattitude	**platitude**	poka	**polka**
plattonic	**platonic**	polen	**pollen**
plattoon	**platoon**	poler	**polar**
plausable	**plausible**	polerise	**polarize**
plazma	**plasma**	poletry	**poultry**
plebbacite	**plebiscite**	polisy	**policy**
plee	**plea**	Pollaris	**Polaris**
pleed	**plead**	Pollaroid	**Polaroid**
pleet	**pleat**	pollemic	**polemic**
pleeze	**please**	pollice	**police**
plege	**pledge**	polligamy	**polygamy**
plenery	**plenary**	pollio	**polio**
plentyful	**plentiful**	pollish	**polish**
plesant	**pleasant**	pollite	**polite**
plesure	**pleasure**	pollitics	**politics**
plethorra	**plethora**	pollyethelene	**polyethylene**
plite	**plight**	pollygon	**polygon**
pluerisy	**pleurisy**	polute	**pollute**
plumer	**plumber**	pome	**poem**
plurel	**plural**		

Incorrect	Correct
pommade	**pomade**
pompidor	**pompadour**
pompus	**pompous**
Pontif	**Pontiff**
pooding	**pudding**
poppular	**popular**
porcelin	**porcelain**
poridge	**porridge**
pornagraphy	**pornography**
porposal	**proposal**
portfollio	**portfolio**
portible	**portable**
portrit	**portrait**
posative	**positive**
posess	**possess**
posession	**possession**
posible	**possible**
pospone	**postpone**
possable	**possible**
possition	**position**
possy	**posse**
postel	**postal**
postige	**postage**
postyure	**posture**
potenshal	**potential**
potery	**pottery**
pottasium	**potassium**
poturri	**potpourri**
pouder	**powder**
pounse	**pounce**
povety	**poverty**
powt	**pout**
poynsetta	**poinsettia**
praier	**prayer**
prairy	**prairie**
praize	**praise**
praktical	**practical**
preceed	**precede**
preceive	**perceive**
precink	**precinct**
precoshious	**precocious**
precure	**procure**
predacate	**predicate**
preddesessor	**predecessor**
predick	**predict**
predictible	**predictable**
predjudice	**prejudice**
preeamble	**preamble**
preech	**preach**
preefabrikate	**prefabricate**
prefeck	**prefect**
preffer	**prefer**
prefice	**preface**
prefrence	**preference**
pregenitor	**progenitor**
pregnent	**pregnant**
preist	**priest**
prelliminary	**preliminary**
prelood	**prelude**
preminent	**preeminent**
premire	**premier**
premiss	**premise**

Incorrect	Correct
premiture	**premature**
premival	**primeval**
premmonition	**premonition**
premyum	**premium**
preocupation	**preoccupation**
preperation	**preparation**
prepetual	**perpetual**
preposal	**proposal**
preppare	**prepare**
prepposition	**preposition**
preprietor	**proprietor**
presadent	**president**
Presbaterian	**Presbyterian**
presedent	**precedent**
preseed	**precede**
presept	**precept**
preshure	**pressure**
preshus	**precious**
presice	**precise**
presipitate	**precipitate**
prespiration	**perspiration**
prespire	**perspire**
pressident	**president**
presstige	**prestige**
prestege	**prestige**
prety	**pretty**
prevade	**pervade**
prevale	**prevail**
prevelant	**prevalent**
previus	**previous**
prevlent	**prevalent**
prevue	**preview**
preycis	**précis**
prezent	**present**
prezide	**preside**
prezident	**president**
prezume	**presume**
prickley	**prickly**
pricless	**priceless**
prie	**pry**
primative	**primitive**
primery	**primary**
prinsess	**princess**
priorty	**priority**
pritify	**prettify**
prity	**pretty**
privaricate	**prevaricate**
priviledge	**privilege**
privisy	**privacy**
privite	**private**
prizm	**prism**
prizon	**prison**
probible	**probable**
problim	**problem**
proccreate	**procreate**
procede	**proceed**
proceedure	**procedure**
procent	**per cent**
proclame	**proclaim**
procter	**proctor**
proddigious	**prodigious**

Incorrect	Correct
proddigy	**prodigy**
produck	**product**
produse	**produce**
profecy	**prophecy**
profer	**proffer**
profeshun	**profession**
proffesor	**professor**
proffess	**profess**
profficient	**proficient**
proffile	**profile**
proffit	**profile**
proflagate	**profligate**
profuce	**profuse**
profunctory	**perfunctory**
proggnosis	**prognosis**
proggres	**progress**
programm	**programme**
prohibbit	**prohibit**
projeck	**project**
projeny	**progeny**
prokrastinate	**procrastinate**
prollific	**prolific**
prologgue	**prologue**
prominade	**promenade**
promisary	**promissory**
prommenade	**promenade**
prommice	**promise**
prommiscuous	**promiscuous**
prommote	**promote**
promt	**prompt**
pronounciation	**pronunciation**
prood	**prude**
proove	**prove**
properganda	**propaganda**
proppagate	**propagate**
proppel	**propel**
propper	**proper**
propperty	**property**
propponent	**proponent**
propportion	**proportion**
proppose	**propose**
propposition	**proposition**
propprietor	**proprietor**
proppultion	**propulsion**
proprity	**propriety**
prosedure	**procedure**
prosess	**process**
prossecute	**prosecute**
prosession	**procession**
prosspect	**prospect**
prosstate	**prostate**
prosstatute	**prostitute**
protatype	**prototype**
proteck	**protect**
protene	**protein**
protude	**protrude**
prottaganist	**protagonist**
prottaplasm	**protoplasm**
prottegay	**protégé**
prottest	**protest**
Prottestent	**Protestant**

Incorrect	Correct
prottocoll	**protocol**
protton	**proton**
provadents	**providence**
provoak	**provoke**
prowd	**proud**
proxxy	**proxy**
prozaic	**prosaic**
psam	**psalm**
psycology	**psychology**
psyconalasis	**psychoanalysis**
publically	**publicly**
publick	**public**
puding	**pudding**
pudjy	**pudgy**
pue	**pew**
pujjy	**pudgy**
pulit	**pullet**
pulkritude	**pulchritude**
pullminary	**pulmonary**
pullpit	**pulpit**
pulverise	**pulverize**
pumkin	**pumpkin**
pumpanickle	**pumpernickel**
punative	**punitive**
punctull	**punctual**
pungture	**puncture**
punjint	**pungent**
punktuate	**punctuate**
punnish	**punish**
pupet	**puppet**
pupull	**pupil**
purchise	**purchase**
purgery	**perjury**
purile	**puerile**
purjery	**perjury**
purpise	**purpose**
pursavere	**persevere**
pursuade	**persuade**
purterb	**perturb**
Purto Rico	**Puerto Rico**
pussilanamous	**pusillanimous**
putred	**putrid**
putrify	**putrefy**
puzzel	**puzzle**
pweblo	**pueblo**
pyaneer	**pioneer**
Pyric victory	**Pyrrhic victory**
pyus	**pious**

Look-Alikes or Sound-Alikes

packed *bundled* • **pact** *agreement*

paean *hymn of joy* • **peon** *peasant*

pail *bucket* • **pale** *enclosure; lacking colour*

pain *ache* • **pane** *window*

pair *two* • **pare** *shave* • **pear** *fruit*

palate *taste* • **palette** *artist's board* • **pallet** *small bed*

pall *covering; gloomy effect* • **Paul** *name*

paltry *few* • **poultry** *fowl*

parish *diocese* • **perish** *die*

parlay *bet* • **parley** *talk*

parley *talk* • **parlay** *bet*

parole *conditional release from prison* • **payroll** *pay*

partition *divider* • **petition** *plea*

passed *did pass* • **past** *former time*

passible *capable of feeling* • **passable** *capable of being passed*

pastoral *rural* • **pastorale** *music*

pastorale *music* • **pastoral** *rural*

pathos *that which incurs pity* • **bathos** *anticlimax*

patience *forbearance* • **patients** *under doctor's care*

pause *delay* • **paws** *touches clumsily; feet* • **pores** *openings*

paw *foot* • **pore** *opening* • **pour** *make flow* • **poor** *not rich*

payroll *pay* • **parole** *conditional release from prison*

peace *no war* • **piece** *portion*

peak *top* • **pique** *anger*

peaked *thin* • **peeked** *looked* • **piqued** *aroused*

peal *bell* • **peel** *strip*

pearl *gem* • **purl** *knitting*

edal *foot lever* • **peddle** *ell*

eeked *looked* • **peaked** *hin* • **piqued** *aroused*

eer *look; equal* • **pier** *dock*

enance *religious* • **ennants** *flags*

endant *ornament* • **endent** *suspended*

endent *suspended* • **endant** *ornament*

ennants *flags* • **penance** *eligious*

eon *peasant* • **paean** *hymn f joy*

perfect *exact* • **prefect** *high fficial*

perish *die* • **parish** *diocese*

persecute *to hound* • **prosecute** *enforce law*

personal *private* • **personnel** *employees*

perspective *vision* • **prospective** *future*

perverse *contrary* • **preserve** *save*

petition *plea* • **partition** *divider*

phantasy *same as* fantasy, *more archaic* • **fantasy** *a far-fetched imaginary idea*

phase *stage* • **faze** *worry* • **fays** *fairies*

phrase *words* • **frays** *battles*

phrenetic *insane* • **frenetic** *frantic*

physic *remedy* • **physique** *body*

physical *body* • **fiscal** *money*

pica *printing measure* • **piker** *cheapskate*

picaresque *rascal* • **picturesque** *colourful*

picture *image* • **pitcher** *vessel; baseball*

picturesque *colourful* • **picaresque** *rascal*

pidgin *the jargon used as a language between foreigners and certain native peoples* • **pigeon** *a bird* • **piggin** *a small wooden pail*

piggin *a small wooden pail* • **pigeon** *a bird* • **pidgin** *the jargon used as a language between foreigners and certain native peoples*

piker *cheapskate* • **pica** *printing measure*

pillar *column* • **pillow** *for head*

pinnacle *peak* • **pinochle** *game of cards*

pinochle *game of cards* • **pinnacle** *peak*

pious *religious* • **Pius** *name of a Pope*

piqued *aroused* • **peaked** *thin* • **peeked** *looked*

pistil *flower* • **pistol** *gun*

Pius *name of a Pope* • **pious** *religious*

plain *simple* • **plane** *smooth; aeroplane*

plaintiff *one who sues* • **plaintive** *sad*

plait *braid* • **plate** *dish*

pleas *legal appeals* • **please** *polite request*

plum *fruit* • **plumb** *line*

poker *cards* • **polka** *dance*

pole *tall wood* • **poll** *vote*

pore *opening; study* • **pour** *with liquid*

poplar *tree* • **popular** *well known*

populace *the masses* • **populous** *thickly inhabited*

porpoise *mammal* • **purpose** *aim*

portend *foretell* • **pretend** *make-believe*

portion *share* • **potion** *dose*

poultry *fowl* • **paltry** *few*

practice *the business of a doctor* • **practise** *to repeat a performance*

pray *say prayers* • **prey** *victim*

precede *go before* • **proceed** *advance*

precedence *priority of rank* • **precedents** *previous laws* • **presidents** *heads of state*

precedent *going before* • **president** *chief official*

precise *accurate* • **précis** *résumé*

precisian *a precise person* • **precision** *accuracy*

precision *accuracy* • **precisian** *a precise person*

prefect *high official* • **perfect** *exact*

prefer *choose* • **proffer** *offer*

preposition *grammar* • **proposition** *offer*

prescribe *give directions* • **proscribe** *to outlaw*

prescription *something ordered* • **proscription** *an imposed restriction*

presence *being present* • **presents**: *verb: to present; gifts*

presentiment *premonition* • **presentment** *presentation*

presents: *verb: to present; gifts* • **presence** *being present*

preserve *save* • **perverse** *contrary*

president *chief official* • **precedent** *going before*

pretend *make-believe* • **portend** *foretell*

pries *opens* • **prize** *award*

principal *chief* • **principle** *axiom; course of conduct*

prints *marks made by pressure* • **prince** *a title of nobility*

prodigy *young genius* • **protégé** *under care*

profit *gain* • **prophet** *one who predicts*

prophecy *noun* • **prophesy** *verb*

proscription *an imposed restriction* • **prescription** *something ordered*

prospective *future* • **perspective** *vision*

pubic *region of body* • **public** *people*

puny *slight* • **puisne** *a junior*

pupil *student* • **pupal** *development stage of larva*

purpose *aim* • **porpoise** *mammal*

put *place* • **putt** *golf*

q

Incorrect	Correct	Incorrect	Correct
quafeur	**coiffure**	questionaire	**questionnaire**
qualefy	**qualify**	quier	**choir**
quallity	**quality**	quik	**quick**
quanity	**quantity**	quivver	**quiver**
quarel	**quarrel**	quizes	**quizzes**
quarentine	**quarantine**	quizical	**quizzical**
quater	**quarter**		

Look-Alikes or Sound-Alikes

quarts *32 ounces* • **quartz** *a mineral*

quay *dock* • **key** *with lock*

quean *female cat; an immoral person* • **queen** *female sovereign*

queerest *strangest* • **querist** *questioner*

queue *line* • **cue** *hint; billiards*

quiet *still* • **quite** *completely, very*

quire *24 sheets* • **choir** *singers*

quote *saying* • **quota** *number*

r

Incorrect	Correct
rabees	**rabies**
rable	**rabble**
rachit	**ratchet**
racizm	**racism**
raddish	**radish**
rade	**raid**
radicle	**radical**
radiel	**radial**
radient	**radiant**
radiod	**radioed**
radyis	**radius**
rafel	**raffle**
raff	**raft**
rafia	**raffia**
raform	**reform**
ragid	**ragged**
raglin	**raglan**
ragoo	**ragout**
rahtha	**rather**
railling	**railing**
raindeer	**reindeer**
rainny	**rainy**
raion	**rayon**
raitable	**ratable**
raivin	**raven**
rajed	**raged**
rajeem	**regime**
rakateer	**racketeer**
raket	**racket**
rakkish	**rakis**
rakontour	**raconteu**
rakoon	**raccoo**
ralie	**rall**
rambil	**rambl**
rameedial	**remedia**
rammafication	**ramificatio**
rammpage	**rampag**
rampint	**rampan**
randim	**randon**
rangle	**wrangl**
ranje	**rang**
rankel	**rankl**
rarety	**rarit**
ransid	**ranci**
ransome	**ranson**
rapayshus	**rapaciou**
rapel	**repe**
rarly	**rarel**
rashio	**rati**
rashnalize	**rationaliz**
rashul	**racia**
rashun	**ratio**
rasser	**razo**
rasy	**rac**
ratal	**rattl**
rath	**wrat**
rattlsnake	**rattlesnak**

Incorrect	Correct
raveel	**reveal**
ravije	**ravage**
ravvil	**ravel**
rawkus	**raucous**
rawr	**raw**
raydium	**radium**
rayment	**raiment**
rayz	**raze**
rayzin	**raisin**
razidjual	**residual**
razzberry	**raspberry**
reakshun	**reaction**
reakter	**reactor**
realaty	**reality**
realese	**release**
realise	**realize**
realy	**really**
reapper	**reaper**
reaserch	**research**
reath	**wreath**
reazon	**reason**
rebell	**rebel**
rebelyon	**rebellion**
rebiuk	**rebuke**
rebutil	**rebuttal**
recalsatrate	**recalcitrate**
recapichulate	**recapitulate**
recclamation	**reclamation**
reccomend	**recommend**
recconoyter	**reconnoitre**
reccord	**record**
reccreation	**recreation**

Incorrect	Correct
reccumpense	**recompense**
recurrance	**recurrence**
receed	**recede**
receit	**receipt**
recepy	**recipe**
reces	**recess**
receshun	**recession**
recievable	**receivable**
recieve	**receive**
reck	**wreck**
recloose	**ecluse**
reconisonce	**reconnaissance**
reconize	**recognize**
recooperate	**recuperate**
recovry	**recovery**
recquire	**require**
recrimnatory	**recriminatory**
recrute	**recruit**
rectafy	**rectify**
rectul	**rectal**
redemshun	**redemption**
reden	**redden**
rediculous	**ridiculous**
redily	**readily**
reduceable	**reducible**
redundent	**redundant**
reduse	**reduce**
redy	**ready**
reech	**reach**
reeder	**reader**

Incorrect	Correct	Incorrect	Correct
reelizm	**realism**	rektangul	**rectangle**
reep	**reap**	rekwital	**requital**
referbish	**refurbish**	rekwizit	**requisite**
reffermation	**reformation**	relaition	**relation**
reffugee	**refugee**	relaks	**relax**
refinment	**refinement**	relavent	**relevant**
refleks	**reflex**	releif	**relief**
reflekshun	**reflection**	releive	**relieve**
refrance	**reference**	relie	**rely**
refrane	**refrain**	relient	**reliant**
refridgerator	**refrigerator**	relinkwish	**relinquish**
refuzal	**refusal**	relitive	**relative**
regail	**regale**	rellegate	**relegate**
reggard	**regard**	rellish	**relish**
regilate	**regulate**	relm	**realm**
reglar	**regular**	relucktinse	**reluctance**
regreshun	**regression**	relyd	**relied**
regretible	**regrettable**	relyible	**reliable**
regul	**regal**	remane	**remain**
regurjatate	**regurgitate**	reme	**ream**
rehabbilitate	**rehabilitate**	remidy	**remedy**
rehearsel	**rehearsal**	reminiss	**reminisce**
reherse	**rehearse**	remishun	**remission**
rejament	**regiment**	remitant	**remittent**
rejensy	**regency**	remitence	**remittance**
rejeuvanate	**rejuvenate**	remmember	**remember**
rejon	**region**	remmit	**remit**
rejoyse	**rejoice**	remnint	**remnant**
rekin	**reckon**	remoat	**remote**
reklis	**reckless**	remonsterate	**remonstrate**
rekoop	**recoup**	remoonerate	**remunerate**
rekord	**record**	remorsful	**remorseful**

Incorrect	Correct
removeable	**removable**
removil	**removal**
renagaid	**renegade**
renaysense	**renaissance**
rendevous	**rendezvous**
reneg	**renege**
renevate	**renovate**
renforce	**reinforce**
rennasonse	**renaissance**
rentry	**re-entry**
renu	**renew**
reorgenise	**reorganize**
reostat	**rheostat**
repare	**repair**
repatishun	**repetition**
repatory	**repertory**
repeel	**repeal**
repelant	**repellent**
reperbate	**reprobate**
repercushin	**repercussion**
reperduce	**reproduce**
reperhensible	**reprehensible**
repersent	**represent**
repetative	**repetitive**
repete	**repeat**
repeun	**repugn**
replacment	**replacement**
replaka	**replica**
repleet	**replete**
replie	**reply**
repozatory	**repository**

Incorrect	Correct
reppakushin	**repercussion**
reppatee	**repartee**
repport	**report**
reppublican	**republican**
reppulshin	**repulsion**
repputible	**reputable**
reprable	**reparable**
repramand	**reprimand**
repreive	**reprieve**
represed	**repressed**
reprizal	**reprisal**
reprize	**reprise**
rerite	**rewrite**
resadense	**residence**
resalution	**resolution**
reseption	**reception**
reserveist	**reservist**
resevation	**reservation**
resevwar	**reservoir**
resind	**rescind**
resint	**recent**
resipracal	**reciprocal**
resiprosity	**reciprocity**
resistence	**resistance**
resitashun	**recitation**
resle	**wrestle**
resorse	**resource**
resparator	**respirator**
respectible	**respectable**
respit	**respite**
responsable	**responsible**
resterant	**restaurant**

Incorrect	Correct	Incorrect	Correct
resteration	**restoration**	revurt	**revert**
resumtion	**resumption**	revvarie	**reverie**
resusitate	**resuscitate**	reyn	**rain**
resytul	**recital**	rezanense	**resonance**
retale	**retail**	rezemblance	**resemblance**
retalliate	**retaliate**	rezent	**resent**
retane	**retain**	rezerve	**reserve**
retch	**wretch**	rezidew	**residue**
retier	**retire**	rezign	**resign**
retirment	**retirement**	rezilyens	**resilience**
retisent	**reticent**	rezin	**resin**
retna	**retina**	rezistable	**resistible**
retorick	**rhetoric**	rezistance	**resistance**
retreive	**retrieve**	reznable	**reasonable**
retrosay	**retroussé**	rezolve	**resolve**
retrospeck	**retrospect**	rezort	**resort**
rettribushun	**retribution**	rezult	**result**
rettrogreshun	**retrogression**	rezume	**resume**
retuch	**retouch**	rezurecshun	**resurrection**
revelle	**reveille**	rhime	**rhyme**
revelution	**revolution**	rhythum	**rhythm**
revenew	**revenue**	ribben	**ribbon**
revenje	**revenge**	ribbuld	**ribald**
revijun	**revision**	ribin	**ribbon**
revilation	**revelation**	richous	**righteous**
revivle	**revival**	richual	**ritual**
revize	**revise**	ridence	**riddance**
revokashun	**revocation**	ridgid	**rigid**
revrent	**reverent**	ridul	**riddle**
revult	**revolt**	rie	**rye**
revursible	**reversible**	rifel	**rifle**
		rigermarole	**rigmarole**

Incorrect	Correct
rigerus	**rigorous**
rigur	**rigour**
riht	**right**
rije	**ridge**
Rik	**Reich**
rikity	**rickety**
rikshaw	**rickshaw**
rilation	**relation**
rilegious	**religious**
rime	**rhyme**
rince	**rinse**
rinestone	**rhinestone**
ringger	**ringer**
rinkle	**wrinkle**
rinocerus	**rhinoceros**
rinseing	**rinsing**
ripal	**ripple**
rippen	**ripen**
ripublic	**republic**
riquire	**require**
riseing	**rising**
riskay	**risqué**
rist	**wrist**
rithe	**writhe**
rithem	**rhythm**
ritten	**written**
riut	**riot**
rivel	**rival**
rivit	**rivet**
rize	**rise**
robbin	**robin**
robery	**robbery**

Incorrect	Correct
rododendrum	
rododendrum	
	rhododendron
roebot	**robot**
roge	**rogue**
rogish	**roguish**
roial	**royal**
rok	**rock**
rokkit	**rocket**
rokoko	**rococo**
rom	**roam**
rong	**wrong**
rooay	**roué**
rood	**rude**
roolet	**roulette**
roon	**ruin**
rooves	**roofs**
roring	**roaring**
rort	**wrought**
rosery	**rosary**
rosey	**rosy**
rost	**roast**
rotery	**rotary**
rotha	**rather**
rotin	**rotten**
roveing	**roving**
royaly	**royally**
roze	**rose**
rozin	**rosin**
rubarb	**rhubarb**
ruber	**rubber**
ruder	**rudder**

Incorrect	Correct	Incorrect	Correct
ruf	**rough**	rupcher	**rupture**
ruge	**rouge**	rurel	**rural**
ruller	**ruler**	ruset	**russet**
rumatism	**rheumatism**	Rusha	**Russia**
rumba	**rhumba**	rusil	**rustle**
rumbil	**rumble**	rustik	**rustic**
rumer	**rumour**	rutine	**routine**
rumije	**rummage**	ryitus	**riotous**
rumy	**rummy**	ryme	**rhyme**
runer	**runner**	rype	**ripe**
runing	**running**	rythm	**rhythm**

Look-Alikes or Sound-Alikes

rabbit *animal* • **rarebit** *food* • **rabid** *fanatical*

rack *shelf* • **wrack** *wreck*

racket *noise* • **racquet** *tennis*

rain *water* • **reign** *rule* • **rein** *on horse*

raise *lift* • **raze** *demolish* • **rays** *light beams*

rap *knock* • **wrap** *fold*

rapped *knocked* • **rapt** *absorbed* • **wrapped** *packed*

read *book* • **reed** *grass* • **red** *colour*

real *actual* • **reel** *wind in; stagger*

realize *understand* • **relies** *counts on*

rebate *deduction* • **rebait** *rehook*

rebound *to spring back* • **redound** *to accrue*

recent *of late* • **resent** *take amiss*

recipe *cookery* • **receipt** *acknowledgment of paying*

redound *to accrue* • **rebound** *to spring back*

reek *vapour* • **wreak** *inflict* • **wreck** *destroy*

referee *arbitrator* • **reverie** *dream*

relater *joiner* • **relator** *narrator*

relic *souvenir of the past* • **relict** *a widow*

respectfully *with esteem* • **respectively** *in the order given*

rest *repose* • **wrest** *pull away*

reveille *signal to awake* • **revelry** *gaiety*

reverend *minister* • **reverent** *respectful*

reverie *dream* • **referee** *arbitrator*

rhyme *poetry* • **rhythm** *metre, beat* • **rime** *frost*

right *correct* • **rite** *ceremony* • **wright** *workman* • **write** *put words on paper*

rime *frost* • **rhyme** *poetry* • **rhythm** *metre, beat*

ring *circle; bell* • **wring** *squeeze*

roam *wander* • **Rome** *city*

roaster *coffee* • **roster** *list*

rock *stone; sway* • **roc** *fabled bird*

rode *did ride* • **road** *path* • **rowed** *boat*

roe *doe; fish egg* • **row** *boating*

role *part* • **roll** *turn around; bread*

Rome *city* • **roam** *wander*

roomer *one who rooms* • **rumour** *gossip*

root *plant* • **route** *way of travel*

rose *flower* • **rows** *lines*

rote *mechanical repetition* • **wrote** *did write*

rough *coarse* • **ruff** *collar; fish; bluster*

rouse *awaken* • **rows** *files; propels by using oars; quarrels*

rung *step; did ring* • **wrung** *squeezed*

rye *grain; alcohol* • **wry** *distorted*

S

Incorrect	Correct	Incorrect	Correct
Sabath	**Sabbath**	sayed	**said**
sabbotage	**sabotage**	scarcly	**scarcely**
sacarin	**saccharin**	scarsity	**scarcity**
sacerfice	**sacrifice**	sceinse	**science**
sacerment	**sacrament**	sceleton	**skeleton**
sacreligous	**sacrilegious**	sceme	**scheme**
safire	**sapphire**	scenry	**scenery**
safty	**safety**	scithe	**scythe**
sakred	**sacred**	scizzers	**scissors**
sakrifice	**sacrifice**	scolastic	**scholastic**
salammi	**salami**	scool	**school**
salery	**salary**	Scripchure	**Scripture**
sallary	**salary**	seceed	**secede**
salm	**psalm**	secertery	**secretary**
Salter	**Psalter**	seduse	**seduce**
sammon	**salmon**	seedan	**sedan**
sanatashun	**sanitation**	seelect	**select**
sandwidge	**sandwich**	seeries	**series**
sargent	**sergeant**	seeson	**season**
sarkastic	**sarcastic**	segragate	**segregate**
sassiety	**society**	seige	**siege**
sassparilla	**sarsaparilla**	seing	**seeing**
Sataday	**Saturday**	seive	**sieve**
satasfactory	**satisfactory**	sekret	**secret**
sattelite	**satellite**	seldem	**seldom**
sattisfaction	**satisfaction**	selebrait	**celebrate**
saught	**sought**	selery	**celery**
sausidge	**sausage**	seleschul	**celestial**
saveing	**saving**	selfs	**selves**

Incorrect	Correct
selibacy	**celibacy**
sellar	**cellar**
sellfish	**selfish**
selluloid	**celluloid**
seme	**seem**
sement	**cement**
semetary	**cemetery**
semmester	**semester**
senater	**senator**
sene	**scene**
senic	**scenic**
sensative	**sensitive**
sentenial	**centennial**
sentor	**centaur**
sentury	**century**
senyer	**senior**
seperate	**separate**
sereal	**cereal**
sereise	**series**
serface	**surface**
sergery	**surgery**
serjon	**surgeon**
sermen	**sermon**
sermize	**surmise**
serplus	**surplus**
serprize	**surprise**
sertificate	**certificate**
servalanse	**surveillance**
servay	**survey**
servicable	**serviceable**
servise	**service**
servive	**survive**

Incorrect	Correct
seseed	**secede**
sesession	**secession**
Setember	**September**
sety	**settee**
seudo	**pseudo**
seudonym	**pseudonym**
sevinth	**seventh**
sevral	**several**
sexsy	**sexy**
sez	**says**
seze	**seize**
shagrin	**chagrin**
shake	**sheik**
shaley	**chalet**
shampain	**champagne**
shamy	**chamois**
shandaleir	**chandelier**
shaperone	**chaperone**
shapo	**chapeau**
sharade	**charade**
sharlatin	**charlatan**
sharliton	**charlatan**
shartroose	**chartreuse**
shartrus	**chartreuse**
shato	**château**
shef	**chef**
sheild	**shield**
sheke	**chic**
shelfish	**shellfish**
shelfs	**shelves**
sheneel	**chenille**
shenyon	**chignon**

Incorrect	Correct	Incorrect	Correct
sheperd	**shepherd**	sillable	**syllable**
sherbert	**sherbet**	sillabus	**syllabus**
sherif	**sheriff**	sillect	**select**
sheth	**sheath**	silouette	**silhouette**
shevron	**chevron**	simbal	**symbol**
shez	**chaise**	simester	**semester**
shicanery	**chicanery**	simetry	**symmetry**
shiek	**sheik**	similer	**similar**
shiffon	**chiffon**	simpathy	**sympathy**
shillaylee	**shillelagh**	simphony	**symphony**
shineing	**shining**	simton	**symptom**
shipd	**shipped**	sinamin	**cinnamon**
shippment	**shipment**	sincerly	**sincerely**
shoffer	**chauffeur**	sinch	**cinch**
sholders	**shoulders**	sinder	**cinder**
shoodn't	**shouldn't**	sindicate	**syndicate**
shouldent	**shouldn't**	sinnic	**cynic**
showvinizm	**chauvinism**	sinse	**since**
shreik	**shriek**	sinsere	**sincere**
shrubry	**shrubbery**	sinthetic	**synthetic**
shud	**should**	sipher	**cipher**
shugar	**sugar**	siramics	**ceramics**
shure	**sure**	sircumstance	**circumstance**
shuv	**shove**	sirrup	**syrup**
sience	**science**	sirynge	**syringe**
sieze	**seize**	sisors	**scissors**
sigar	**cigar**	sist	**cyst**
sigarette	**cigarette**	sistem	**system**
siggnificant	**significant**	sistern	**cistern**
signerture	**signature**	sitadel	**citadel**
sikada	**cicada**	sittuation	**situation**
silance	**silence**		

Incorrect	Correct
sixt	**sixth**
sizm	**schism**
skarce	**scarce**
skare	**scare**
skeme	**scheme**
skeptical	**sceptical**
skism	**schism**
skool	**school**
skooner	**schooner**
slayed	**slain**
slax	**slacks**
sodder	**solder**
sofemore	**sophomore**
sofen	**soften**
sofer	**sofa**
sofisticate	**sophisticate**
solem	**solemn**
soler	**solar**
sollid	**solid**
sophmore	**sophomore**
sorce	**source**
sord	**sword**
sorow	**sorrow**
sory	**sorry**
soshalist	**socialist**
sosiety	**society**
sothern	**southern**
sourkraut	**sauerkraut**
sovrin	**sovereign**
Sowvyet Union	**Soviet Union**
spagetti	**spaghetti**

Incorrect	Correct
Spanyerd	**Spaniard**
speach	**speech**
speshialty	**specialty**
speshul	**special**
spesify	**specify**
spesiman	**specimen**
spirrit	**spirit**
sponser	**sponsor**
sprily	**spryly**
stanch	**staunch**
starberd	**starboard**
stateing	**stating**
statis	**status**
statment	**statement**
stattistic	**statistic**
stawk	**stalk**
stedy	**steady**
stelthy	**stealthy**
stomick	**stomach**
stoped	**stopped**
storey	**story**
stories	**storeys**
straight-jacket	**straitjacket**
strech	**stretch**
strenth	**strength**
strenyous	**strenuous**
stricly	**strictly**
strugle	**struggle**
studdy	**study**
studeying	**studying**
stuped	**stupid**

Incorrect	Correct	Incorrect	Correct
subburban	**suburban**	supplys	**supplies**
suberb	**suburb**	supprise	**surprise**
subordnate	**subordinate**	supress	**suppress**
subscribtion	**subscription**	suprintendent	**superintendent**
subsistance	**subsistence**	suround	**surround**
succede	**succeed**	survise	**service**
succeser	**successor**	suspishon	**suspicion**
sucsess	**success**	sutle	**subtle**
sufferage	**suffrage**	suvenir	**souvenir**
suffishent	**sufficient**	suvvival	**survival**
suficient	**sufficient**	swade	**suede**
sufix	**suffix**	swair	**swear**
suger	**sugar**	swave	**suave**
sugjest	**suggest**	syche	**psyche**
sujjest	**suggest**	sychiatrist	**psychiatrist**
sujjestion	**suggestion**	sychic	**psychic**
suksinct	**succinct**	sychology	**psychology**
sumary	**summary**	sychosis	**psychosis**
summarine	**submarine**	sygnificant	**significant**
supena	**subpoena**	sykey	**psyche**
supercede	**supersede**	symetrical	**symmetrical**
suply	**supply**	symtom	**symptom**
supose	**suppose**	synic	**cynic**
supperfluous	**superfluous**		

Look-Alikes or Sound-Alikes

sac *baglike part of animal or plant* • **sack** *bag*

saccharin *sweetener* • **saccharine** *very sweet*

sail *on boat* • **sale** *sell at low price*

salvage *to save from wreckage* • **selvage** *the edge of woven fabric*

sanitary *hygienic* • **sanatory** *healing*

Satan *devil* • **satin** *fabric* • **sateen** *cotton fabric resembling satin*

satire *wit used to ridicule* • **satyr** *a sylvan deity or demigod*

saviour *one who saves* • **Saviour** *Christ*

scene *place* • **seen** *did see*

scents *smells* • **sense** *brains* • **cents** *money*

schilling *Austrian coin* • **shilling** *old British coin*

scrip *money* • **script** *story*

sculptor *one who carves* • **sculpture** *work of sculptor*

sea *water* • **see** *vision*

sealing *closing* • **ceiling** *top of room*

seam *line* • **seem** *appear*

sear *burn* • **seer** *prophet*

seas *bodies of water* • **seize** *grab* • **sees** *observes*

secede *withdraw* • **succeed** *to accomplish*

seed *flower* • **cede** *give up*

sell *opposite of buy* • **cell** *prison; in biology*

seller *one who sells* • **cellar** *basement*

selvage *the edge of woven fabric* • **salvage** *to save from wreckage*

senior *older* • **señor** *mister*

senses *sight, touch* • **census** *population count*

sent *dispatched* • **scent** *perfume*

serf *slave* • **surf** *sea*

serge *fabric* • **surge** *swell*

serial *in a row* • **cereal** *food*

session *meeting* • **cession** *yielding*

settler *colonist* • **settlor** *one who makes a legal settlement*

sever *cut* • **severe** *strict*

sew *stitch* • **so** *like this* • **sow** *plant*

shake *disturb* • **sheik** *Arab chief*

shear *clip* • **sheer** *thin*

sheriff *county officer* • **sherif** *Arab prince*

shilling *old British coin* • **schilling** *Austrian coin*

shirt *garment* • **chert** *a rock*

shoe *footwear* • **shoo** *go away*

shone *did shine* • **shown** *did show*

shoot *fire* • **chute** *drop*

shriek *cry out* • **shrike** *bird*

sic *thus* • **sick** *ill*

Sicilian *from Sicily, an island off and part of Italy* • **Cilician** *from Cilicia, a province in Asia Minor*

side *next to* • **sighed** *did sigh*

sighs *sound* • **size** *bigness*

sight *see* • **site** *place* • **cite** *point out*

sign *symbol; put name on* • **sine** *mathematics*

signet *a seal* • **cygnet** *a young swan*

singeing *burning* • **singing** *song*

singing *song* • **singeing** *burning*

skull *head* • **scull** *boat*

slave *one who has lost his freedom* • **Slav** *one who speaks a Slavic language as his native tongue*

slay *kill* • **sleigh** *sled*

sleight *trick* • **slight** *small; snub*

sloe *plum* • **slow** *not fast*

soar *rise* • **sore** *aching*

sodality *a fellowship* • **solidarity** *union*

sold *did sell* • **soled** *put on a sole*

soldier *military* • **solder** *to fuse*

sole *fish; shoe* • **soul** *spirit*

some *a few* • **sum** *total*

someone *some person* • **some one** *one of several*

son *child* • **sun** *sky*

sooth *truth* • **soothe** *calm*

sort *species* • **sought** *looked for*

special *particular, specific* • **especial** *exceptional, preeminent*

specialty *an employment limited to one kind of work* • **speciality** *quality of being special*

specie *coin* • **species** *variety*

staid *sober* • **stayed** *remained*

stair *to climb* • **stare** *look steadily*

stake *post; gamble* • **steak** *food*

stalk *stem of plant; walk stealthily* • **stork** *bird*

stationary *fixed* • **stationery** *paper supplies*

statue *sculpted figure* • **stature** *height* • **statute** *law*

steal *rob* • **steel** *metal*

step *pace* • **steppe** *plain*

stile *step* • **style** *fashion*

stork *bird* • **stalk** *stem of plant; walk stealthily*

story *tale* • **storey** *floor of a building*

straight *direct* • **strait** *body of water*

stricture *binding* • **structure** *form*

structure *form* • **stricture** *binding*

style *fashion* • **stile** *step*

suburb *near city* • **superb** *very good*

succour *help* • **sucker** *fool*

suit *clothes* • **suite** *rooms* • **sweet** *sugary*

sum *total* • **some** *a few*

summary *brief account* • **summery** *fit for summer*

sundae *ice-cream* • **Sunday** *Sabbath*

superb *very good* • **suburb** *near city*

surplice *church garment* • **surplus** *left over*

symbol *sign* • **cymbal** *music*

t

Incorrect	Correct
tabblet	**tablet**
tabbulate	**tabulate**
tabu	**taboo**
tafeta	**taffeta**
tailer	**tailor**
tante	**taint**
takeing	**taking**
takkle	**tackle**
takt	**tact**
taktics	**tactics**
tallent	**talent**
tangable	**tangible**
tanjent	**tangent**
tanntalize	**tantalize**
tanntrum	**tantrum**
targit	**target**
tarmiggan	**ptarmigan**
tarrif	**tariff**
tarrnish	**tarnish**
tassit	**tacit**
tasteing	**tasting**
tatered	**tattered**
tatle	**tattle**
tatoo	**tattoo**
taudry	**tawdry**
teara	**tiara**
tecksture	**texture**
tecnical	**technical**
teech	**teach**
teenadger	**teenager**
teen's	**teens**
teer	**tier**
teerful	**tearful**
tejious	**tedious**
tekela	**tequila**
teknik	**technique**
tekstile	**textile**
telagram	**telegram**
telavision	**television**
tellephone	**telephone**
tellevision	**television**
temmerity	**temerity**
temmplit	**template**
temp	**tempt**
temperarily	**temporarily**
temperment	**temperament**
temprary	**temporary**
temprature	**temperature**
temprence	**temperance**
temt	**tempt**
temtation	**temptation**
tenament	**tenement**
tenasity	**tenacity**
tendancy	**tendency**
tenden	**tendon**
tenent	**tenant**
tener	**tenor**

Incorrect	Correct
Tenesee	**Tennessee**
enible	**tenable**
enit	**tenet**
ennacious	**tenacious**
enndenshous	**tendentious**
ennsion	**tension**
ennuous	**tenuous**
enticle	**tentacle**
entitive	**tentative**
eppee	**tepee**
eppid	**tepid**
erane	**terrain**
eratory	**territory**
erestrial	**terrestrial**
terible	**terrible**
terific	**terrific**
terify	**terrify**
eritorial	**territorial**
terpentine	**turpentine**
terpitude	**turpitude**
terrer	**terror**
terribally	**terribly**
testafy	**testify**
testamony	**testimony**
testiment	**testament**
Teusday	**Tuesday**
texbook	**textbook**
theem	**theme**
theeology	**theology**
theerum	**theorem**
thef	**theft**
theif	**thief**
their's	**theirs**
theirselves	**themselves**
theiter	**theatre**
themselfs	**themselves**
theriputic	**therapeutic**
thermanooklear	**thermonuclear**
thermistat	**thermostat**
thersty	**thirsty**
therteen	**thirteen**
thery	**theory**
thesirus	**thesaurus**
thesus	**thesis**
theze	**these**
thiefs	**thieves**
thogh	**though**
thoro	**thorough**
thousind	**thousand**
thred	**thread**
threshhold	**threshold**
thret	**threat**
thriftey	**thrifty**
thriling	**thrilling**
thriveing	**thriving**
throte	**throat**
thugg	**thug**
thum	**thumb**
thwort	**thwart**
Thyland	**Thailand**
tickel	**tickle**
tieing	**tying**
til	**till**

Incorrect	Correct
timerity	**temerity**
timmerous	**timorous**
timmid	**timid**
tiney	**tiny**
tingel	**tingle**
tinje	**tinge**
tinn	**tin**
tinnsel	**tinsel**
tipe	**type**
tippoff	**tip-off**
tirant	**tyrant**
tirms	**terms**
tite	**tight**
tittalate	**titillate**
tittle	**title**
tittular	**titular**
tobbaco	**tobacco**
tobogun	**toboggan**
to-day	**today**
todey	**toady**
togga	**toga**
toggether	**together**
toilit	**toilet**
tokin	**token**
tole	**toll**
tollerant	**tolerant**
tomaine	**ptomaine**
tommorow	**tomorrow**
tomoroe	**tomorrow**
tonage	**tonnage**
tonnic	**tonic**
tonnsil	**tonsil**

Incorrect	Correc
toogether	**togethe**
toolip	**tuli**
toom	**tom**
toomstone	**tombston**
toonight	**tonigh**
toor	**tou**
Toosday	**Tuesda**
toothe	**toot**
topick	**topi**
toppic	**topi**
tora	**Tora**
torador	**toreado**
torement	**tormen**
torenado	**tornad**
torepedo	**torped**
torid	**torri**
torint	**torrer**
tork	**torqu**
torper	**torpc**
totling	**totallin**
tousand	**thousan**
tradegy	**traged**
transferr	**transfe**
transsfer	**transfe**
traser	**trace**
trechery	**treacher**
tresurer	**treasure**
trimendous	**tremendou**
tripple	**tripl**
tripplecate	**triplicat**
trist	**trys**
truble	**troubl**

Incorrect	Correct	Incorrect	Correct
truefully	**truthfully**	turmite	**termite**
truely	**truly**	turms	**terms**
tryed	**tried**	turse	**terse**
tryumph	**triumph**	twealth	**twelfth**
tummul	**tumult**	twelth	**twelfth**
tumor	**tumour**	tympany	**timpami**
tung	**tongue**	typeriter	**typewriter**
tunnage	**tonnage**	tyrade	**tirade**
turminate	**terminate**	tythe	**tithe**
turminel	**terminal**	Tywan	**Taiwan**

Look-Alikes or Sound-Alikes

tacked *fastened* • **tact** *consideration*

tacks *fasteners* • **tax** *money paid government*

tail *end* • **tale** *story*

talc *powder* • **talk** *speak*

taper *candle; narrow* • **tapir** *animal*

tarantella *dance* • **tarantula** *spider*

tare *weight* • **tear** *rip*

tartar *on teeth; chemical* • **tartare** *sauce* • **Tartar** *a people*

taught *did teach* • **taut** *tense*

tax *money paid government* • **tacks** *fasteners*

tea *drink* • **tee** *golf*

team *group* • **teem** *swarm*

tear *crying* • **tier** *layer*

teas *drinks* • **tease** *annoy*

technics *technical rules* • **techniques** *manners of performance*

techniques *manners of performance* • **technics** *technical rules*

teeth *plural of tooth* • **teethe** *to grow teeth*

tenant *renter* • **tenet** *belief*

tenor *singer* • **tenure** *duration*

tern *bird* • **turn** *rotate*

than *as in 'greater than'* • **then** *at that time*

their *belong to them* • **there** *that place* • **they're** *they are*

thence *from that time or place* • **hence** *from this time or place*

therefor *for that, for it, for them, etc.* • **therefore** *for this reason*

therefore *for this reason* • **therefor** *for that, for it, for them, etc.*

thrash *to swing or strike* • **thresh** *to beat out grain*

threw *tossed* • **through** *penetrated; finished*

throe *pang* • **throw** *hurl*

throne *king* • **thrown** *tossed*

throw *hurl* • **throe** *pang*

tic *twitching* • **tick** *pillow; clock*

tide *ocean* • **tied** *connected*

timber *wood* • **timbre** *tone*

tinny *like tin* • **tiny** *small*

tiny *small* • **tinny** *like tin*

to *towards* • **too** *also* • **two** *number*

toe *foot* • **tow** *pull*

toiled *worked* • **told** *said* • **tolled** *bell*

toilet *bathroom* • **toilette** *grooming attire*

told *said* • **toiled** *worked* • **tolled** *bell*

tomb *grave* • **tome** *book*

ton *weight* • **tun** *large cask*

tongue *in mouth* • **tong** *too*

topee *sun-helmet* • **toupee** *hairpiece for man*

topography *maps, charts* • **typography** *printing*

ortious *legal term referring o tort* • **tortuous** *twisting* • **orturous** *painful*

oupee *hairpiece for man* • **opee** *sun-helmet*

our *trip* • **tower** *building*

rack *path* • **tract** *region; amphlet*

rail *path* • **trial** *court*

ray *salver* • **trait** *haracteristic*

treaties *agreements* • **treatise** *account*

troop *soldiers* • **troupe** *actors*

tuba *musical instrument* • **tuber** *root of plant*

turban *head-covering* • **turbine** *power*

typography *printing* • **topography** *maps, charts*

u

Incorrect	Correct
ubbiquitous	**ubiquitous**
ucharist	**Eucharist**
uge	**huge**
ugenics	**eugenics**
ukalalee	**ukulele**
ulltimite	**ultimate**
ulltirior	**ulterior**
ulogy	**eulogy**
ulser	**ulcer**
ultamatum	**ultimatum**
umane	**humane**
umberella	**umbrella**
umble	**humble**
umbridge	**umbrage**
umility	**humility**
ummbillical	**umbilical**
ummpire	**umpire**
umpopular	**unpopular**
unalatteral	**unilateral**
unamed	**unnamed**
unanamus	**unanimous**
unason	**unison**
Untarian	**Unitarian**
unatural	**unnatural**
unaverse	**universe**
unawganized	**unorganized**
unconsolable	**inconsolable**
undaprivilledged	**underprivileged**

Incorrect	Corre
undataker	**undertake**
unddress	**undres**
undeground	**undergroun**
underiter	**underwrite**
underrite	**underwrit**
undigestible	**indigestibl**
undinyable	**undeniabl**
undisirable	**undesirabl**
undoo	**undu**
undoubtably	**undoubtedl**
unduely	**undul**
undyeing	**undyin**
uneek	**uniqu**
uneiform	**unifor**
unempeachible	**unimpeachabl**
unerned	**unearne**
unerth	**uneart**
unescapable	**inescapabl**
unesessary	**unnecessar**
unezy	**uneas**
unfagetible	**unforgettabl**
unfare	**unfai**
unfinnished	**unfinishe**
unfitt	**unfi**
unfotunate	**unfortunat**
unfrendly	**unfriendl**
unfrequent	**infrequen**
ungoddly	**ungodl**

Incorrect	Correct
ungreatful	**ungrateful**
unhelthy	**unhealthy**
unholey	**unholy**
unick	**eunuch**
unifey	**unify**
uniquivikal	**unequivocal**
unitey	**unity**
Unitid Stats	**United States**
univercity	**university**
universly	**universally**
unkemp	**unkempt**
unkle	**uncle**
unkonditionel	**unconditional**
unkonscious	**unconscious**
unkooth	**uncouth**
unkshus	**unctuous**
unncommon	**uncommon**
unnequil	**unequal**
unnering	**unerring**
unnerstand	**understand**
unnfavrable	**unfavourable**
unnit	**unit**
Unnited Nashuns	**United Nations**
unnocupied	**unoccupied**
unnowable	**unknowable**
unnpregudiced	**unprejudiced**
unnprincipaled	**unprincipled**
unplesent	**unpleasant**
unpresidented	**unprecedented**
unredeemable	**irredeemable**
unsertin	**uncertain**
untill	**until**
unumployed	**unemployed**
urb	**herb**
useable	**usable**
usefull	**useful**
useing	**using**
use to	**used to**
usualy	**usually**
usurpor	**usurper**

Look-Alikes or Sound-Alikes

udder *part of cow* • **utter** *speak*

umpire *referee* • **empire** *dominion*

unable *not able* • **enable** *to make able*

unique *sole* • **eunuch** *sexless*

urbane *courteous* • **urban** *town*

urn *vase* • **earn** *gain; to receive a salary*

utter *speak* • **udder** *part of a cow*

V

Incorrect	Correct	Incorrect	Correct
vaccilate	**vacillate**	vegitible	**vegetable**
vacinnation	**vaccination**	vegitibul	**vegetable**
vacume	**vacuum**	vehamint	**vehement**
valer	**valour**	vehimint	**vehement**
valintine	**valentine**	veicle	**vehicle**
vallid	**valid**	velosity	**velocity**
valuble	**valuable**	venam	**venom**
valv	**valve**	Veneetion	**Venetian**
vanaty	**vanity**	vengance	**vengeance**
vandel	**vandal**	venil	**venal**
vandle	**vandal**	venim	**venom**
vaneer	**veneer**	venimus	**venomous**
vanesh	**vanish**	Veniss	**Venice**
vannila	**vanilla**	venorashun	**veneration**
vantrillokwist	**ventriloquist**	venorible	**venerable**
		ventellacion	**ventilation**
vantriloquist	**ventriloquist**	ventellate	**ventilate**
		venttullation	**ventilation**
vaped	**vapid**	ventullation	**ventilation**
vassel	**vassal**	venul	**venal**
Vatecan	**Vatican**	venum	**venom**
vaze	**vase**	venumus	**venomous**
veanul	**venal**	verafiable	**verifiable**
vecablerry	**vocabulary**	verafucation	**verification**
vecks	**vex**	verafy	**verify**
vecter	**vector**	verafyible	**verifiable**
veenel	**venal**	veraly	**verily**
vegetible	**vegetable**	verassity	**veracity**
vegitable	**vegetable**	veraty	**verity**

Incorrect	Correct
verbil	**verbal**
verbily	**verbally**
verble	**verbal**
verbul	**verbal**
verbully	**verbally**
verchu	**virtue**
vergin	**virgin**
veriaty	**variety**
verible	**variable**
verilaty	**virility**
verious	**various**
verius	**various**
vermen	**vermin**
vermooth	**vermouth**
vermuth	**vermouth**
vernackuler	**vernacular**
vernackular	**vernacular**
versafy	**versify**
versas	**versus**
versefacation	**versification**
versefecation	**versification**
versifucation	**versification**
versitil	**versatile**
versufy	**versify**
versutil	**versatile**
vertabra	**vertebra**
vertabrate	**vertebrate**
vertabril	**vertebral**
vertibrate	**vertebrate**
vertibrul	**vertebral**
verticle	**vertical**
vertiu	**virtue**
vertubra	**vertebra**
vertue	**virtue**
verufyible	**verifiable**
veruly	**verily**
veruty	**verity**
veryous	**various**
vesinity	**vicinity**
vesle	**vessel**
vessal	**vessel**
vessul	**vessel**
vestabule	**vestibule**
vestabyul	**vestibule**
vestad	**vested**
vestage	**vestige**
vestid	**vested**
vestitch	**vestige**
vestubyule	**vestibule**
vetaranery	**veterinary**
veterinary	**veterinary**
Vet Nam	**Vietnam**
vetos	**vetoes**
vetrans	**veterans**
vibrent	**vibrant**
vibrunt	**vibrant**
victam	**victim**
victem	**victim**
victer	**victor**
victom	**victim**
victry	**victory**

Incorrect	Correct	Incorrect	Correct
victum	**victim**	visiate	**vitiate**
vieing	**vying**	visige	**visage**
viel	**veil**	visinnity	**vicinity**
vien	**vein**	visuge	**visage**
vigar	**vigour**	vitaman	**vitamin**
vigel	**vigil**	vitel	**vital**
vigelence	**vigilance**	vitelly	**vitally**
viger	**vigour**	vitely	**vitally**
vigourous	**vigorous**	vitle	**vital**
vigur	**vigour**	vittles	**victuals**
vilage	**village**	vitul	**vital**
vilense	**violence**	vitully	**vitally**
villege	**village**	viuble	**viable**
vilet	**violet**	vivad	**vivid**
villify	**vilify**	vivod	**vivid**
villige	**village**	vizable	**visible**
villin	**villain**	vizor	**visor**
vinagar	**vinegar**	vodvil	**vaudeville**
vindacate	**vindicate**	volentary	**voluntary**
vindecate	**vindicate**	volyum	**volume**
vinear	**veneer**	vomet	**vomit**
vineer	**veneer**	vomut	**vomit**
vinella	**vanilla**	vosiferus	**vociferous**
violon	**violin**	voyce	**voice**
vipar	**viper**	voys	**voice**
vipur	**viper**	vulger	**vulgar**
virtebrate	**vertebrate**	vuntrilloquist	**ventriloquist**
virulance	**virulence**	vurnaculer	**vernacular**
virulant	**virulent**	vurs	**verse**
virulunt	**virulent**	vursatil	**versatile**
viscious	**vicious**	vurses	**verses**
vise	**vice**		

Incorrect	Correct	Incorrect	Correct
vursification	**versification**	vurtue	**virtue**
vursus	**versus**	vusanity	**vicinity**
vurtabra	**vertebra**	vyabel	**viable**

Look-Alikes or Sound-Alikes

vacation *rest* • **vocation** *job*

vain *proud* • **vane** *weather* • **vein** *blood*

valance *drapery* • **valence** *in chemistry, degree of combining power*

vale *valley* • **veil** *face covering*

valence *in chemistry, degree of combining power* • **valance** *drapery*

venal *corruptible* • **venial** *excusable*

veracity *truth* • **voracity** *hunger*

veracious *truthful* • **voracious** *greedy*

verses *poetry* • **versus** *against*

vial *glass* • **vile** *loathsome* • **viol** *music*

vice *depraved* • **vise** *hold*

Volga *Russian river* • **vulgar** *crude, impolite*

voracity *hunger* • **veracity** *truth*

w

Incorrect	Correct
wafur	**wafer**
waggon	**wagon**
wakon	**waken**
wallnut	**walnut**
wallut	**wallet**
wantin	**wanton**
wantun	**wanton**
warbel	**warble**
warbil	**warble**
warbul	**warble**
wardan	**warden**
wardon	**warden**
wardun	**warden**
warrantee	**warranty**
warreor	**warrior**
warriur	**warrior**
waryer	**warrior**
wasteage	**wastage**
waylayed	**waylaid**
wearhouse	**warehouse**
weary	**wary**
weding	**wedding**
wellcome	**welcome**
wellfare	**welfare**
welth	**wealth**
Wensday	**Wednesday**
weppon	**weapon**
werld	**world**
wership	**worship**
werth	**worth**
wery	**wary**
westurn	**western**
wether	**weather**
wether	**whether**
whisle	**whistle**
wiald	**wild**
wickad	**wicked**
wickud	**wicked**
wield	**wild**
wierd	**weird**
wifes	**wives**
wilderniss	**wilderness**
wildurnes	**wilderness**
wildurniss	**wilderness**
wile	**while**
wimmen	**women**
wins	**wince**
wipperwill	**whippoorwill**
wisedom	**wisdom**
wisk	**whisk**
wisky	**whisky**
wisper	**whisper**
wite	**white**
withar	**wither**
withold	**withhold**
withur	**wither**
wiuld	**wild**
wizzard	**wizard**

Incorrect	**Correct**	Incorrect	**Correc**
wolfs	**wolves**	wossel	**wassai**
wonderous	**wondrous**	wot	**wha**
wonst	**once**	wresle	**wrestl**
woom	**womb**	writeing	**writin**
woosted	**worsted**	wun	**wo**
worning	**warning**	wund	**woun**
worp	**warp**	wurld	**worl**
worrysome	**worrisome**	wurm	**worn**

Look-Alikes or Sound-Alikes

wade *walk through water* • **weighed** *did weigh*

wain *farm wagon* • **wane** *fade*

wail *cry* • **whale** *mammal*

waist *body* • **waste** *unused*

wait *stay for* • **weight** *heaviness*

waive *give up* • **wave** *water; gesture*

waiver *surrender claim* • **waver** *falter*

war *combat* • **wore** *past tense of wear*

ward *hospital* • **warred** *fought*

ware *goods* • **wear** *clothes* • **where** *which place?* • **were** *verb*

way *direction* • **weigh** *pounds* • **whey** *milk*

we *us* • **wee** *tiny*

weak *feeble* • **week** *seven days*

weal *wound* • **we'll** *we will* • **wheel** *round body*

weather *atmosphere* • **whether** *if* • **wether** *sheep*

welch *cheat* • **Welsh** *from Wales*

wet *water* • **whet** *appetite*

which *what one?* • **witch** *hag*

Whig *political party* • **wig** *hair*

while *during* • **wile** *trick*

whine *complain* • **wine** *drink*

whither *where* • **wither** *decay*

whole *complete* • **hole** *opening*

wholly *fully* • **holey** *having holes* • **holy** *religious*

whoop *yell* • **hoop** *circle*

whore *prostitute* • **hoar** *white with age or frost*

who's *who is* • **whose** *to whom*

won *did win* • **one** *single*

wont *habit* • **won't** *will not*

wood *timber* • **would** *might*

wore *past tense of wear* • **war** *combat*

wrap *fold* • **rap** *knock*

wrapped *packed* • **rapt** *absorbed* • **rapped** *knocked*

wreak *inflict* • **wreck** *destroy* • **reek** *vapour*

wreath *flowers* • **wreathe** *twist*

wreck *ship* • **reck** *care*

wrest *pull away* • **rest** *repose*

wretch *despicable person; pitied for misfortune* • **retch** *vomit*

wright *workman* • **write** *put words on paper* • **right** *correct* • **rite** *ceremony*

wring *squeeze* • **ring** *circle; bell*

wrote *did write* • **rote** *mechanical repetition*

wrung *squeezed* • **rung** *step; did ring*

wry *distorted* • **rye** *grain; alcohol*

xyz

Incorrect	Correct
xlyaphone	**xylophone**
Xmass	**Xmas**
y'all	**you all**
yeild	**yield**
yeller	**yellow**
yerself	**yourself**
yestaday	**yesterday**
yestiday	**yesterday**
yesturday	**yesterday**
yodal	**yodel**
yogart	**yogurt** (or: yoghurt)
yogee	**yogi**
yogert	**yogurt** (or: yoghurt)
yogu	**yoga**
yoman	**yeoman**
yondar	**yonder**
yondur	**yonder**
yot	**yacht**
youngstor	**youngster**
youngstur	**youngster**
your's	**yours**
yungster	**youngster**
Zar	**Czar**
Zavier	**Xavier**
zeel	**zeal**
zeenith	**zenith**
zefir	**zephyr**
zefur	**zephyr**
zenon	**xenon**
zepher	**zephyr**
zink	**zinc**
zithar	**zither**
zithur	**zither**
zodeac	**zodiac**
zoolegy	**zoology**
Zus	**Zeus**
Zuse	**Zeus**
zylophone	**xylophone**

Look-Alikes or Sound-Alikes

yawl *sailboat* • **yowl** *loud cry*

yaws *tropical disease* • **yours** *possessive of you*

yew *tree* • **you** *person* • **ewe** *sheep*

yoke *frame for animals* • **yolk** *egg*

you'll *you will* • **Yule** *Christmas*

your *belongs to you* • **you're** *you are*

yours *possessive of you* • **yaws** *tropical disease*

yowl *loud cry* • **yawl** *sailboat*

QUICK LIST OF CORRECT SPELLINGS

a

aardvark
Aaron
abandon
abbreviate
abdomen
ability
able
abolition
abrupt
absence
absent
absenteeism
absolutely
absurd
abuse
abyss
academic
accede
accelerate
accent
access
accessible
accessory
accident
accidentally
acclaim
acclimatize
accommodate
accompany
accomplice
accomplish
accord
according
accordion
accost
account
accountant
accredit
accrue
accumulate
accuracy
accurate
accuse
accustom
ace
ache
achieve
acid
acknowledge
acne
acoustics
acquaintance
acquiesce
acquire
acquisition
acquit
acquittal
acre
acreage
acrobat
across
acrostic
actor
actual
actually
acumen
acute
adage
adamant
addict
addition
address
adequate
adequately
adhere
adjacent
adjoining
adjourn
adjustable
adjutant
administration
administrator
admirable
admiral
admissible
admission
admit
admittance
adolescence
adolescent
adopt
adorable
adult
advance
advantage
advantageous
advertise
advertisement
advisable
adviser
advisory
advocate
aerial
aerodynamics
aeronautics
aeroplane
aerosol
affable
affair
affect
affidavit
affiliate
affirm
affix
afflict
affluence
afford
affront
Afghan
afraid
Africa
afterwards
against
aged
ageing
agencies
agency
agenda
aggrandize
aggravate
aggregate
aggressive
aghast
agitator
agrarian
agree
agreeable
agreeing
agricultural
agriculture
aground
aisle
alcohol
alert
alibi
alien
align
allege
allegiance
allergy
alleviate

alley
alliance
allocate
allot
allotment
allotted
allotting
allow
allowance
allowed
all right
ally
almanac
almighty
almond
almost
alone
alphabet
already
also
alternate
although
altogether
altruism
aluminium
always
amateur
ambassador
ambidextrous
ambiguous
ambulance
ameliorate
amenable
amend
amendment
American
amiable
amity
ammonia
ammunition
among
amorous
amount
amour
amusement
analogue
analogy
analyse
analysis
ancestor
ancestry
anchor
anchovy
ancient
anecdote
anew
ankle
annex
annihilate
anniversary
annotate
announcement
annoyance
annual
annually
annuity
annul
anoint
anonymous
another
answer
antarctic
antecedent
antenna
antibiotic
anti-British
anticipate
antidote
antique
antiseptic
anxiety
anxious
any
any time
anywhere
apartment
aperture
aphorism
apologetically
apologies
apologize
apology
apostle
apostrophe
appalling
apparatus
apparel
apparent
appeal
appear
appearance
appease
appellate
appendectomy
appendix
appetite
applaud
appliance
applicant
applies
apply
appoint
appointee
appraisal
appraise
appreciable
appreciate
apprehend
apprentice
approach
appropriate
approve
approximate
apricot
apron
apropos
aptitude
aqueduct
arbitrary
arbitrate
archaic
architect
archives
arctic
area
arguing
argument
arise
arising
arithmetic
armada
armful
armistice
around
arouse
arousing
arraign
arrange
arrangement
arrears
arrest
arrival
arrive
arrogant
arrow
artery
article
artificial
artillery
artistically
ascend
ascertain
ashen
Asia
asinine
asked
asphalt
aspirant
aspirin
assail
assassin
assassinate
assault
assemble
assent
assert

assess
asset
assign
assimilable
assist
assistance
assistant
associate
assort
assuage
assume
assurance
assure
asthma
astronaut
asylum
ate
atheist
athlete
athletic
atmosphere
attach
attack
attacked
attain
attempt
attend
attendance
attendant
attention
attest
attic
attire
attitude
attract
auctioneer
audible
audience
auditorium
August
au revoir
authentic
author
authority
authorize
automatic
automatically
automation
automobile
autumn
auxiliary
available
avalanche
average
aviator
avid
avoidable
awe
awful
awkward
axis

b

bacchanal
bachelor
background
backward
bacon
bade
badge
bagel
baggage
balance
balk
ballad
ballet
ballistics
ballot
balmy
banana
bandage
banister
banjos
bankrupt
bankruptcy
banner
baptize
barbecue
bargain
barley
barracks
barrage
barrel
barricade
basic
basically
basis
bastard
baste
battalion
battery
beacon
beautician
beautiful
beauty
beaver
because
become
becoming
beetle
before
began
beggar
begin
beginner
beginning
beguile
behaviour
beige
belief
believe
belittle
belligerent
bely
beneath
beneficial
beneficiary
benefit
benefited
benevolent
bent
berate
berserk
besiege
bestial
betray
better
beware
beyond
Bible
biceps
bicycle
bier
bigamy
biggest
bigot
bilious
billet
billiard
billion
binary
binoculars
biography
birch
bird
birdie
biscuit
bisect
bitter
bivouac
blackguard
blameful
blameless
blanket
blare
blasé
blasphemy
bleach
bleak
blessed
blight
blithe
blitz
blizzard
block
blockade

blotter
blouse
bludgeon
bluff
board
boast
boatswain
body
boisterous
bolster
bomb
bonfire
bonnet
bonus
bony
bookkeeping
borrow
bosom
bossy
botch
bottle
bottom
boudoir
bought
bouillon
boulevard
boundary
bouquet
bourbon
bourgeois
boycott
bracelet
braggart
braid
brain
brake
brand-new
brassiere
bravery
brazen
breadth
break
breakable
breakfast
breast
breed
breeze
brethren
bridge
brief
brigadier
bright
brilliant
Britain
Britannica
British
broccoli
broken
brokerage
bronchial
brook
browse
bruised
bucket
buckle
Buddha
budge
budget
buffalo
buffer
buffet
buffoon
bugle
build
built
bulldozer
bullet
bulletin
bumblebee
bungalow
bunion
buoy
buoyant
burden
bureau
burglary
burial
burst
busily
business
bustle
busybody
butcher
button
buxom

C

cabbage
cabinet
cable
cache
cactus
cadet
café
caffeine
calamity
calcium
calf
calibre
calico
California
calk
callisthenics
calm
calves
calypso
calorie
camaraderie
camel
camellia
camera
camisole
camouflage
campaign
camphor
campus
Canada
canal
canapé
cancel
cancer
candidate
candle
candour
canine
canister
canker
cannery
cannibal
canoe
canopy
cantaloup
cantilever
canvas
canyon
capable
capacious
capacity
capillary
capital
capitulate
caprice
capsule
captain
caption
carafe
caramel
carat
carbohydrate
carburettor
cardiac
cardinal
career
careful
caress
Caribbean
caricature
caring
carnal
carnival
carouse
carriage
carried
carrot
carrying
carte blanche

cartel
cartilage
carton
cartoon
cartridge
cascade
casement
cashew
cashier
cashmere
casket
casserole
cassock
castanet
caste
castigate
castle
casualty
cataclysm
catacomb
catalogue
catapult
cataract
catarrh
catastrophe
catch
category
caterpillar
cathedral
catholic
caucus
cauliflower
caulk
cause
caustic
caution
cautious
cavalcade
cavalier
cavernous
cease
cedar
ceiling
celebrate
celery
celestial
celibacy
cellar
cello
cellophane
celluloid
Celtic
cement
cemetery
census
centaur
centennial
central
centrifugal
century
ceramics
cereal
cerebral
ceremony
certain
certificate
chafe
chagrin
chagrined
chain
chair
chaise
chalet
chalk
challenge
chameleon
champagne
champion
chandelier
changeable
channel
chaos
chapeau
chaperon
chaplain
character
charade
chariot
charity
charlatan
chartreuse
chasm
chaste
château
chatter
chauffeur
chauvinism
cheap
cheat
Cheddar
cheer
cheese
chef
chemical
chemist
chenille
cherub
chestnut
chevron
chic
Chicago
chicanery
chief
chieftain
chiffon
chignon
children
chimney
chinchilla
chintz
Chippendale
chiropody
chisel
chivalrous
chlorine
chloroform
chocolate
choice
choir
cholera
choreography
chorus
chow mein
christen
Christian
Christmas
chromatism
chrome
chronic
chubby
chummy
cicada
cider
cigar
cigarette
cinch
Cincinnati
cinder
cinnamon
cipher
circle
circuit
circular
circumcise
circumstance
cistern
citadel
citation
citizen
citrus
civil
civilization
clairvoyance
clamour
clammy
clannish
claque
classify
clause
cleanse
clearance
cleavage
clerical
clerk
clientele
cliff

climb
clipper
clique
cloak
cloche
clock
cloister
closet
closure
clothes
clown
clumsy
coach
cobweb
coercion
coffee
coffin
cogitate
cognac
coherent
coiffure
coincidence
colander
coleslaw
colic
Coliseum
collaborate
collapse
collapsible
collar
collateral
colleague
collect
collector
college
collegiate
colloquial
cologne
colonel
colonnade
coloratura
colossal
Colosseum
colour
column
columnist
comb
comedian
comedy
comet
comfortable
comic
coming
comma
command
commemorate
commence
commendable
commensurate
commercial
commission
commit
committed
committee
commodity
common
communicate
communism
communist
community
commute
companion
comparable
comparative
compass
compatible
compel
compelled
compensation
compete
competence
competent
competition
complexion
compliance
complicate
compose
composition
compressed
compromise
comptroller
compulsory
comrade
conceal
concede
conceit
conceive
concentrate
concentric
concept
concert
concession
conciliate
concise
conclave
concoct
concourse
concrete
concur
concurrence
concussion
condemn
condensation
condescend
condition
conduct
confectionery
confederate
conference
conferred
confess
confidence
confinement
confirm
conflagration
Confucius
congeal
congenial
congratulate
congregation
congruous
conjecture
conjugate
conjure
connect
connection
connoisseur
connotation
connote
connubial
conquer
conscience
conscientious
conscious
consensus
consequence
conservatory
consider
considerable
consignment
consistent
console
consolidate
constable
constant
constellation
consul
consummate
consumption
contagious
contain
contemplate
contemporary
contempt
contemptible
continent
continually
continuous
contour
contractual
contrariwise
contrary
contretemps
contribute
control
controlled

controversial
convalesce
convenient
converge
converse
convertible
convolute
convulse
cookery
coolly
cooper
cooperate
coordination
Copenhagen
copious
copyright
copywriter
coral
cordage
cordial
corduroy
corkage
corned beef
corner
cornice
coronary
coroner
corporal
corporation
corps
corpuscle
corral
corralled
correct
correlate
correspond
correspondence
corridor
corroborate
corrugated
corrupt
corsage
corset
cosmic
cosmopolitan
Cossack
cosy
cotillion
cottage
cotton
cough
counsellor
countenance
counterfeit
countess
country
coup de grace
coupé
couple
coupon
courage
courier
court
courteous
courtesan
courtesy
courtmartial
cousin
covenant
cover
coverage
coward
coxswain
coyly
coyote
crabby
crack
crackle
cradle
craft
cranberry
crane
crawl
crayon
cream
crease
creation
creature
credence
credential
credible
credulous
crepe
crescendo
crew
cricket
cried
criminal
crimson
cripple
critical
criticize
critique
crochet
crocodile
croquet
croquette
croupier
crowd
crowned
crucial
crude
cruel
cruelly
cruelty
cruiser
crumb
crutch
cry
cryptic
crystallize
Cuba
cuckoo
cudgel
culinary
culture
cunning
cupboard
curfew
curiosity
curly
currency
current
curriculum
currier
cursed
curtain
curve
custard
custody
customer
cultivate
cycle
cyclone
cylinder
cynic
cyst
Czar

d

dabble
dachshund
dacron
daffodil
dagger
dahlia
daily
daiquiri
dairy
damage
dandelion
dandruff
dangerous
data
daughter
dauphin
dawdle
dazzle
deacon
dead
deaf
dealt
debate
debaucher
debonair
debris

bt
but
cade
ceased
ceit
ceive
ecember
cent
cibel
cided
ciduous
cimal
cipher
cision
claration
cline
écolleté
ecorate
ecrease
edicate
educe
eductible
efault
efeat
efence
efendant
efensible
eference
eferred
efiance
eficient
eficit
efied
efinite
efinitely
efy
ehydrate
eign
elegate
eliberate
elicacy
elicatessen
elicious
elight

delinquent
delivery
deluge
delusion
deluxe
demagogue
dementia
praecox
demi-tasse
democracy
democrat
demolish
demonstrable
demonstrate
denial
dense
dental
dentifrice
dentist
deny
deodorant
departure
dependable
dependent
deplete
deplete
deposit
depravation
deprivation
deprive
depths
deputy
derelict
derive
derogative
derrick
descend
describe
description
desecrate
desegregate
desertion
desiccate
design

desirable
desolate
despair
desperate
despicable
destination
destroy
destruction
detail
detect
detergent
deteriorate
determine
deterrent
destable
deuce
devastate
develop
device
devil
devious
devise
devoid
devotion
dextrous
diabetes
diagnose
dialect
diamond
diaper
diaphragm
diarrhoea
diary
dichotomy
dictionary
didn't
die
diesel
dietary
dietitian
difference
differential
difficult
diffuse

digest
digestible
digging
digitalis
digressive
dilapidated
dilemma
diligent
dilute
dimension
diminish
diminutive
dining
dinner
dinosaur
diocese
diphtheria
diploma
dire
direction
dirge
disagreement
disallow
disappear
disappoint
disarray
disastrous
disbursement
discard
discern
disciple
discipline
discommodity
disconcert
disconsolate
discount
discourteous
discover
discrepancy
discriminate
discuss
discussion
disdain
disease

disguise
dishonest
disillusion
dismantle
dismiss
dismissal
disparage
dispensary
disperse
displacement
disposable
disposal
dispossess
disproportion
dispute
disqualify
disreputable
disrupt
dissatisfy
dissect
disseminate
dissent
dissident
dissimilar
dissipate
dissociate
dissolve
dissonant
dissuade
distaff
distance
distasteful
distillation
distinct
distinguish
distraught
distress
distribute
district
disturb
ditto
divan
diverge
divert
dividend
divine
divorce
divulge
docile
doctor
doctrinaire
documentary
dodge
does
doggerel
doldrums
dollar
dolphin
domicile
dominant
domineer
dominion
domino
donkey
donor
don't
doom
door
dormant
dormitory
dosage
dossier
double
doubt
dough
doughnut
dove
dovetail
dowager
dowdy
dozen
dragon
drainage
drama
drawn
dread
dream
dreary
dredge
dress
dried
driftwood
drill
drink
drive-in
driveway
drizzle
droll
dromedary
droop
dropping
drowned
drowse
drudgery
druggist
drunkenness
dry
dual
dubious
dulcet
dullness
duly
dunce
dungaree
dungeon
duplex
duplicate
duplicity
durable
duress
during
Dutch
dutiful
dwarf
dying
dynamic

e

eager
eagle
earl
earlier
early
earnest
earring
earth
easement
easily
Easter
easy
eaves
ebony
ebullient
eccentric
ecclesiastical
echo
eclipse
economic
ecstasy
ecumenical
eczema
edge
edible
edition
editor
educable
educate
eel
effect
effervescent
efficacious
efficiency
effort
egg
ego
eighteen
eighth
either
eject
elaborate
elbow
elect
electricity
elegant
elegy
element

lementary
lephant
leven
lf
licit
licit
ligible
liminate
lite
lixir
llipse
lm
loquent
lucidate
lude
lves
lse
manate
mbalm
mbarrassed
mbellish
mbezzle
mblem
mboss
mbrace
mbroider
mbryo
merald
mergency
migrant
minence
missary
mollient
motion
mperor
mphasis
mpire
mployee
mptiness
mpty
nable
namoured
nchant
nclosure
encompass
encore
encourage
encroach
encyclopedia
endear
endeavour
endorsement
endowment
endurance
enemy
energetic
enervate
enforce
enforceable
engagement
engine
engineer
England
English
engrave
enhance
enjoyment
enlighten
enliven
en masse
enmesh
enmity
ennoble
enormous
enough
enquire
enrage
enrapture
enrich
en route
ensemble
ensign
entail
entangle
enterprise
entertain
enthusiasm
entice
entire
entomology
entourage
entrance
entreat
entrée
entrepreneur
entry
enunciate
envelop
envelopes
enviable
envies
environment
envy
enwrap
epic
epicure
epidemic
episode
epitaph
epoch
equally
equilibrium
equinox
equipped
equity
equivalent
erase
erection
ermine
errand
erratic
erroneous
error
erudite
escalator
escort
Eskimo
espionage
essay
essential
establish
estimate
etch
eternity
ethical
etiquette
Eucharist
eugenics
eulogy
eunuch
euphemism
European
evening
every
everywhere
evidence
evil
evolution
exact
exactly
exaggerate
exalt
examination
example
exasperate
exceed
excel
excellent
except
excessive
excise
excitable
excitement
exclude
excruciate
excursion
execute
executive
exercise
exert
exhale
exhaust
exhibit
exhilarate
exile
exist

existence
exodus
exonerate
exorbitant
exotic
expel
expendable
expense
experience
expiration
explanation
expletive
explicit
exposal
express
extemporaneou
extension
extinct
extracurricular
extraordinary
extravagant
extreme
extricate
extrovert

f

fable
fabric
fabulous
façade
face
facetious
facial
facilitate
facing
facsimile
fact
faction
factor
factory
factual
faculty
Fahrenheit
fail
faille
faint
fairly
faith
falcon
fall
fallacy
fallible
false
falsetto
falsify
fame
familiar
family
famine
famous
fanatic
fanciful
far
farce
farm
farther
fascinate
fashion
fasten
fatal
fateful
fathom
fatigue
fatten
fatuous
faucet
fault
favourable
fawn
fear
feasible
feast
feather
feature
February
federal
feebly
feel
feign
felicitate
fell
fellow
felony
felt
feminine
fence
ferment
ferocious
ferry
fertile
festival
fetch
fetter
feud
feudal
fever
few
fiasco
fibrous
fickle
fiddle
fidelity
fidget
field
fiend
fierce
fiery
fight
figure
file
Filipino
film
filter
final
finance
financial
finely
finesse
finger
fire
firing
firm
first
fission
fix
flabbergast
flaccid
flagging
flagrant
flake
flame
flammable
flapper
flatten
flatter
flatulent
flavour
flaw
flea
fledgling
fleece
fleet
flesh
flexible
flicker
flies
flight
flimsy
flippant
flirt
flirtatious
float
flock
flood
floor
florist
flotilla
flounce
flounder
flourish
flower
flown
fluent
fluid
fluorescent
fluoride

ute
y
am
cal
cus
e
ggy
ld
liage
lk
llow
lly
ment
ndle
nt
otball
rbid
rcible
recast
recastle
reclose
regone
rehead
reign
reman
remost
resee
resight
rest
rever
rfeit
rge
rgery
rget
rgive
rk
rmal
rmally
rmer
rmidable
rmula
rsake
rsythia
rtitude

fortune
forty
forum
forward
fossil
fought
found
fountain
fourteen
fourth
fox
fragrance
frail
frame
fraternal
fraudulent
fraught
freak
freckle
freight
frequency
freshen
Freud
friar
fricassee
friction
Friday
friend
fright
fringe
frivolous
frock
frontal
frontiersman
frontispiece
frown
frozen
frugal
fruitful
fuchsia
fudge
fugitive
fugue
fulfil

fumble
fume
function
fundamental
funeral
fungus
funnel
furious
furlough
furnish
furniture
furry
further
fuselage
futile
future

g

gabardine
gadget
galaxy
gale
gallant
gallery
Gallic
gallon
gallop
gallows
gamble
game
gamut
gangrene
garage
garbage
garden
gardener
garlic
garret
garrulous
gas
gaseous
gasket
gasoline
gauche

gauge
gauze
gazelle
gazette
gear
geezer
geisha
gelatine
gendarme
genealogy
generally
generous
genetic
genial
genius
gentile
gentleman
gently
genuine
Georgia
geriatrics
German
germane
gesture
geyser
ghastly
ghetto
ghost
giant
giddy
gigantic
giggle
gigolo
gimmick
ginger
gingham
girdle
girl
giraffe
giveaway
glacial
glamorous
glance
glare

glass
glazier
gleam
glider
glimmer
glimpse
glitter
global
gloom
glorify
glossary
glutton
glycerine
gnarl
gnash
gnat
gnaw
gnome
goad
goal
gobble
goblet
goddess
gondola
gone
good
goose
gopher
gorgeous
gospel
gossamer
gossip
gourd
gourmet
government
governor
gown
graceful
gracious
grade
gradual
grain
grammar
grand
grandeur
graph
grass
grateful
gratitude
gravel
gravity
grease
greedy
green
greet
grenade
greyhound
grief
grievance
grieve
grille
grimace
groan
grocery
grope
gross
grotesque
group
grovel
grudge
gruesome
guarantee
guard
guess
guest
guidance
guide
guileless
guinea
guitar
gullible
gunner
gurgle
gutter
guttural
guy
gymnasium
gynaecology
gyp
gypsum
gypsy
gyroscope

h

haberdasher
habilitate
habituate
hacienda
hack
haddock
haemoglobin
haemorrhage
haemorrhoids
haggard
haggle
halcyon
half
hallelujah
hallow
Halloween
hallucinate
halo
halves
hamburger
hamlet
hammer
handful
handicap
handkerchief
handle
happen
happily
harangue
harass
harbour
hardboiled
hardening
harebrained
harem
harlequin
harmonious
harness
harridan
harried
harsh
harvest
hassle
hasten
hatch
hatchet
hate
haughty
haunt
haven
Hawaii
hay
hazard
hazel
head
headache
headdress
health
heap
hearse
hearth
heartily
hearty
heat
heathen
heave
heaven
heavy
heckle
hectic
hedge
hedonist
heifer
height
heinous
heiress
heirloom
helicopter
hell
hello
helmet
hemisphere

henceforth
henna
herald
herb
herbaceous
heredity
hereon
heresy
heretofore
heritage
heroes
hermitage
herring
hers
hesitate
heterogeneous
hexagon
hiatus
hibernate
hickory
hidden
hideous
hierarchy
hieroglyphic
highbrow
highness
hilarious
hindrance
hindsight
hinge
hippopotamus
hireling
history
hitch
hoax
hobby
hockey
hodgepodge
hoist
holiday
holiness
hollandaise
hollow
holocaust

homage
home
homely
homemaker
homestead
homicide
homogeneous
honest
honey
honeydew
honour
honourable
honorary
hood
hoof
hook
hoping
horizon
hormone
hornet
horoscope
horrendous
horrible
horrified
horror
hors d'oeuvres
horse
horsy
horticulture
hose
hosiery
hospital
hostage
hostile
hotel
hound
household
houses
housewife
housing
hovel
hover
howl
huddle

huge
humane
humble
humiliate
humility
humming
humorous
humour
hundred
hunger
hungry
hunting
hurdle
hurl
hurray
hurricane
hurriedly
husband
hussy
hustle
hybrid
hydrangea
hydrant
hydraulic
hydrogen
hydrophobia
hyena
hygiene
hymnal
hypertension
hyphen
hypnotist
hypocrisy
hypocrite
hypodermic
hypothetical
hysteria

i

ibex
ice
iceberg
Iceland
ichthyology

icing
icon
iconoclast
idea
ideal
identical
identify
ideology
ides
idiom
idiosyncrasy
idiot
idolater
idyllic
ignominious
ignorant
ignore
iguana
Iliad
illegal
illegible
illegitimate
illicit
illiterate
illogical
illuminate
illusion
illustrate
image
imaginable
imagination
imagine
imbecile
imbibe
imbue
imitation
immaculate
immaterial
immature
immeasurable
immediate
immemorable
immense
immigrant

imminent
immobile
immoral
immortal
immune
impair
impartial
impasse
impassioned
impatient
impeach
impeccable
impecunious
impede
impel
impenetrable
imperial
impersonal
imperturbable
impetus
impiety
impinge
impious
implacable
implement
implicit
imply
impolite
importance
impossibility
impotent
impresario
impress
impression
impromptu
improvement
impugn
inaccurate
inane
inappropriate
inapt
inaugurate
inauspicious
incalculable
incandescent
incarnate
incendiary
incentive
incessant
incest
incident
incidentally
incriminator
incipient
inclement
inclination
include
incognito
inconsolable
incorporate
incorrigible
increase
incredible
increment
incumbent
incurred
incurring
indebted
indecent
indecorous
indefensible
indelible
independent
index
Indian
indicative
indictment
indifferent
indigenous
indigestible
indigo
indiscriminate
individually
indoctrinate
indolent
indomitable
inducement
inebriate
ineffable
inefficacious
inefficient
inert
inertia
inescapable
inevitable
inexorable
infallible
infamous
infancy
infant
infection
inference
inferior
infidelity
infiltrate
infinitely
infinitive
infirmary
inflammable
inflation
inflection
influence
information
infrared
infrequent
infuriate
infuse
ingenious
ingratiate
ingredient
inhabitant
inhale
inherit
inhibition
initial
initiative
injection
injury
injustice
innate
inner
innervate
innocence
innocuous
innovate
innuendo
inoculate
inordinate
inquire
insanity
inscrutable
insect
inseparable
inside
insight
insipid
insistent
insolent
insoluble
inspiration
instance
instantaneous
instead
instigate
instinct
institute
instrument
insubordinate
insufferable
insulate
intangible
integral
integrate
intellectual
intelligence
intemperate
intensify
intention
intercede
intercept
intercession
intercourse
interest
interesting
interfere
interference

interlude
intermediate
intermittent
internal
interpolate
interpret
interrogate
interrupt
interview
intimate
intoxicate
intricacy
intrigue
introduce
invalid
invasion
inveigle
investigate
inveterate
invigorate
invisible
invite
invoice
invoke
inward
iodine
irascible
iridescence
iron
irrational
irreconcilable
irredeemable
irregular
irrelevance
irrelevant
irresistible
irresponsible
irrevocable
irrigate
irritable
Islam
island
isle
isolate
isotope
Israel
issuance
issue
isthmus
Italian
itch
item
ivory
ivy

j

jackal
jackass
jacket
jackknife
jade
jagged
jaguar
jail
jalopy
janitor
January
Japanese
jardiniere
jargon
jasmine
jaundice
jazz
jealous
jeep
jeer
jelly
jeopardy
jerk
jersey
Jesuit
jettison
jewellery
jewels
jibe
jigger
jitterbug
jobber
jockey
jocular
jodhpurs
joker
jolly
jostle
jotting
journal
journey
jovial
joyous
jubilant
jubilee
judge
judgment
judicial
judiciary
jugger
juice
juncture
jungle
junior
jurisdiction
jury
just
justice
justify
juvenile

k

kaleidoscope
kangaroo
kaput
kayak
keel
keen
kennel
kept
kerchief
kernel
kerosene
kettle
key
khaki
kibitzer
kick
kidney
killer
kilowatt
kimono
kindergarten
kindness
kindle
kindred
kingdom
kipper
kissed
kitchen
kitten
kleptomania
knack
knapsack
knee
knick-knack
knife
knives
knob
knock
knoll
knotted
knout
knowledge
knuckle
kosher
Kremlin

l

label
laboratory
labour
labyrinth
lace
lacerate
lachrymose
lacing
lackey
laconic
lacquer

ladder
ladies
ladle
laggard
lagging
laid
lake
lambaste
lame
lamentable
laminate
lance
ländler
landlord
landscape
language
languish
languor
lanolin
lantern
lapel
larceny
large
larkspur
larynx
lascivious
lassie
lassitude
lasso
latch
late
lately
latent
latitude
latticework
laudable
laughable
laughter
launch
laundry
laurel
lavatory
lavender
lawn
lawyer
laxative
laziness
leader
leaf
league
leakage
leapt
learn
lease
leather
leave
leaven
leaves
lecture
ledger
legal
legalize
legend
legerdemain
legging
legible
legion
legislature
legitimate
leisure
leisurely
lemonade
length
lenient
lens
lent
leopard
leprechaun
leprosy
lesbian
lethal
lethargy
let's
letter
lettered
lettuce
letup
level
leveller
lévitation
lewd
lexicon
liability
liaison
liar
libel
liberal
liberalism
libidinous
libido
library
libretto
licentious
licorice
Liebfraumilch
liege
lieu
lieutenant
lifeboat
lifetime
likeable
likely
likeness
lilac
lily
limb
limber
lime
limelight
limit
linear
linen
lingerie
linguist
linkage
limousine
linoleum
lion
liquefy
liquid
liquor
lissome
listen
literacy
little
liturgical
livelihood
lively
livery
lives
lizard
loafer
loathe
lobby
localize
locket
locomotive
locust
lodge
logarithm
logic
loneliness
lonely
longevity
longitude
loquacious
lord
lore
Lorelei
lorgnette
lose
loss
lotion
lottery
loud
lounge
lousy
louvre
Louvre
lovable
love
lovely
loving
lowbrow
loyal
lubricate

lucid
luck
ludicrous
luggage
lukewarm
lullaby
luminescent
lunacy
lunatic
lure
luscious
lustrous
lute
luxuriant
luxury
lying
lymph
lynx
lyric

m

macadam
macaroni
macaroon
machete
Machiavellian
machinery
mackerel
mackintosh
madame
mademoiselle
madras
magazine
maggot
magic
magistrate
magnet
magnificence
magnitude
maharajah
mahogany
maidenly
maintenance
maître d'
major
majority
making
malady
malediction
malfeasance
malice
malign
malinger
malleable
mammal
mammoth
manacle
manageable
manager
mandatory
mange
manger
mania
manicure
manifesto
manifold
manner
manoeuvre
mansion
mantelpiece
manufacture
many
maple
maraschino
maraud
marble
margarine
margin
marijuana
marine
maritime
market
marmalade
maroon
marquis
marquise
marriage
marriageable
married
marrow
marry
martini
martyr
marvellous
masculine
masonry
masquerade
massacre
masseur
massive
master
masticate
material
maternity
mathematics
matinée
matriarch
matronly
matter
mattress
maturation
mature
maudlin
mausoleum
maverick
maximum
maybe
mayonnaise
meadow
meager
meanness
meant
measles
measure
mechanic
mechanize
medal
medallion
meddle
medicine
medieval
mediocre
Mediterranean
medium
medley
megalomania
melancholy
mélange
melon
mellow
melodious
melodrama
membrane
memento
memoir
memorable
memorial
memory
menace
menagerie
menial
menstruate
mental
mention
menu
mercenary
merchandise
mercy
merely
merger
meringue
merit
merrily
messenger
mesmerize
messy
metal
metallic
metamorphosis
metaphor
meteor
Methodist
metropolitan
mezzanine
miasma
mice

microscope
midday
middle
mien
migrate
mileage
military
militia
millennium
millinery
millionaire
mince
mineral
mingle
miniature
minimum
minister
minority
minus
minuscule
minute
minutiae
miracle
mirage
mirror
miscellaneous
mischief
mischievous
misconduct
miser
miserable
misery
misfortune
mishap
mislaid
misogyny
missile
mission
Mississippi
misspell
misstate
mistake
mistress
mitten

mixture
mnemonic
moan
moat
mobilize
moccasin
mockery
model
modern
modest
modifier
modulate
moire
moisture
molecule
molestation
mollify
momentous
monarch
monastery
money
monkey
monogamist
monopoly
monotone
monotonous
monsieur
monstrous
month
mope
morality
morgue
Mormon
Morocco
morphine
morsel
mortally
mortgage
mortify
mortuary
mosaic
mosque
mosquito
mossy

motif
motion
motor
mottled
mournful
moustache
movable
movement
mucilage
mucous
mucus
muddy
Muhammadan
mulatto
mulish
multiply
mundane
murderer
murmur
muscle
museum
music
muslin
mustard
mutiny
myopia
myrtle
mysterious
mystery
mysticism
mystify
mythical

n

nagged
nail
naïve
naïveté
naked
nameless
naphtha
narcissistic
narcotics
narration

narrow
nascent
nastiness
nasturtium
national
naturally
nature
nausea
navigable
navy
near
neat
nebulous
necessary
necessity
neck
neckerchief
necromancy
nectarine
needle
nefarious
negative
neglect
negligée
negligence
negotiate
neighbour
neither
nephew
nepotism
nervous
nestle
neuralgia
neuritis
neurologist
neurotic
neutral
neutralize
new
next
Niagara
nibble
nicely
niche

ickel
icotine
iece
ight
ihilism
il
imble
ineteen
inety
inth
ipple
obleman
oblesse oblige
octurnal
oise
oisome
ominate
onchalant
onentity
ormal
orth
ortherly
osegay
ostalgic
otable
otary
otch
othing
otice
oticeable
otion
otorious
ourish
ouveau riche
novel
novice
nowhere
noxious
nuclear
nucleus
nudity
nuisance
nullification
numb
numerous
numskull
nunnery
nuptial
nurse
nursemaid
nurseries
nutrition
nutty
nymph

O

oar
oath
obbligato
obedience
obese
obey
obituary
object
objectionable
oblige
oblique
obnoxious
obscene
obsequious
observance
obsession
obsolescent
obsolete
obstacle
obstetrician
obstinate
obvious
occasion
occasional
occupancy
occupant
occupied
occur
occurrence
ocean
oceanography
octopus
oculist
odd
odorous
odour
Odyssey
Oedipus
off
offence
offer
offering
office
official
officious
often
ogle
ogre
oil
ointment
old
olfactory
olive
Olympic
omelette
ominous
omissible
omission
omit
omniscient
omnivorous
once
onerous
opaque
open
openness
opera
operate
operator
operetta
ophthalmology
opinion
opium
opponent
opportune
opportunity
oppose
oppressor
optician
optional
optimism
opus
oracle
orange
orator
orbit
orchestra
orchid
ordinary
ordinance
organ
organization
orgasm
orgy
origin
original
ornament
orphan
orthodox
oscillate
osculatory
ossify
ostensible
ostentatious
ostrich
ought
ounce
ours
ourselves
oust
outer
outrageous
outsider
outward
ovary
overrate
overreach
overrun
overseer
overt

overture
overwhelm
overwrought
oxygen
oyster

p

Pacific
pacifist
pacify
package
pact
padre
paean
pageant
pagoda
paid
paisley
Pakistan
palace
palatable
palate
palatial
palisade
pallbearer
palm
palmistry
palpable
palpitate
palsy
pamphlet
panacea
panatella
pancake
pandemonium
panel
panicky
panorama
pansy
pantomime
papacy
papier-mâché •
paprika
parable
parabola
parachute
parade
paradise
paradox
paraffin
paragraph
parakeet
parallel
paralyse
paralysis
paramecium
paramount
paranoia
paraphernalia
paraphrase
paraplegic
parasite
paratrooper
parcel
parenthesis
parfait
pari-mutuel
parish
parity
parliament
parlour
Parmesan
parochial
parody
parole
parquet
parrot
parsley
parson
partial
participate
participle
particle
particular
parties
partisan
partition
partitive
partner
passable
passage
passé
passion
passive
passport
pastel
pasteurize
pastime
pasting
pastor
pastrami
pastry
pâté de foie gras
patent
paternal
pathos
patient
patio
patriot
patriotism
patrol
patron
pattern
pavement
pavilion
paving
peach
peanut
peas
peasant
pecan
peccadillo
peculiar
pecuniary
pedestal
pedestrian
pediatrics
pedigree
peevish
peignoir
pellet
pell-mell
penal
penalty
pencil
pendulum
penetrate
penicillin
peninsula
penitent
penitentiary
penknife
penmanship
pennant
penniless
Pentagon
Pentecostal
penurious
people
per annum
perceive
per cent
percolator
percussion
perennial
perfect
perforate
perform
perfunctory
perhaps
peril
perimeter
period
periphery
periscope
perish
perjury
permanent
permeate
permissible
permit
peroxide
perpendicular
perpetrate
perpetual

persecute
persevere
persistence
person
personal
perspicacious
perspiration
perspire
persuade
pertinent
perturb
pervade
perverse
pervert
peso
pessimist
pesticide
petal
petite
petition
petrify
petroleum
petticoat
petulant
pew
phantom
pharaoh
pharmacy
phase
phenobarbital
phenomenon
philanderer
philanthropy
philately
philharmonic
Philippines
philosophy
phlegm
phobia
phoenix
phonetic
phonics
phonograph
phony
phosphate
phosphorus
photograph
phrase
physically
physician
physics
physiognomy
physiology
physiotherapy
physique
pianist
piano
piazza
pica
picayune
piccolo
picket
pickle
picnic
piece
pierce
piety
pigment
pilfer
pilgrim
piling
pillage
pillar
pillbox
pillory
pilot
pimento
pimple
pincers
pineapple
pinnacle
pinup
pioneer
pious
piping
pistachio
piston
pitfall
pitiful
pittance
pituitary
pivot
pizza
placard
placate
placebo
placement
placid
plagiarism
plague
plaid
planet
planetarium
plasma
plastic
plateau
platform
platinum
platitude
platonic
platoon
platter
plausible
plaza
plea
plead
pleasant
please
pleasure
pleat
plebiscite
pledge
plenary
plentiful
plethora
pleurisy
pliable
pliers
plight
plumber
plural
plus
plutonium
pneumatic
pneumonia
pocket
pocketbook
poem
poet
pogrom
poignant
poinsettia
poise
poison
polar
Polaris
polarize
Polaroid
polemic
police
policy
polio
polish
polite
politics
polka
pollen
pollute
polyethylene
polygamy
polygon
pomade
pompadour
pompous
Pontiff
popular
porcelain
pornography
portable
portfolio
portrait
position
positive
posse
possess
possession

possible
postage
postal
postpone
posture
potato
potassium
potential
potpourri
pottery
poultry
pounce
pour
pout
poverty
powder
practical
prairie
prayer
preamble
precarious
precaution
precede
precedent
precept
precinct
precious
precipitate
précis
precise
preclude
precocious
predecessor
predicament
predicate
predict
predictable
predominant
preeminent
prefabricate
preface
prefer
preference
pregnant
prejudice
preliminary
prelude
premature
premier
premise
premium
premonition
preoccupation
preparation
prepare
preponderant
preposition
preposterous
prerogative
Presbyterian
prescribe
prescription
present
preserve
preside
president
pressure
prestige
presume
presumption
pretend
prettify
pretty
prevail
prevalent
prevaricate
prevention
preview
previous
priceless
prickly
priest
primary
primeval
primitive
princess
priority
prism
prison
privacy
private
privilege
probable
problem
procedure
proceed
process
procession
proclaim
procrastinate
procreate
proctor
procure
prodigious
prodigy
produce
product
profess
profession
professor
proffer
proficient
profile
profit
profligate
profuse
progenitor
progeny
prognosis
programme
progress
prohibit
project
prolific
prologue
promenade
promiscuous
promise
promissory
prompt
pronunciation
propaganda
propel
proper
property
prophecy
prophet
proponent
proportion
proposal
propose
proposition
proprietor
propriety
propulsion
prosaic
prosecute
prospective
prospectus
prostate
prostitute
protagonist
protect
protégé
protein
protest
Protestant
protocol
proton
protoplasm
prototype
protrude
proud
prove
provide
providence
provoke
proximity
proxy
prude
pry
psalm
pseudo
pseudonym
psyche
psychology

sychosis
tomaine
ublic
udding
udgy
ueblo
uerile
uerto Rico
ulchritude
ullet
ulmonary
ulpit
ulverize
umpernickel
umpkin
unctual
unctuate
ungent
unitive
uppet
urchase
ure
urge
urple
urpose
urse
pursue
pursuit
pusillanimous
putrefy
putrid
putt
puzzle
pyjamas
pyramid
Pyrex
pyromaniac
pyrotechnics
Pyrrhic victory

q

qualify
quality
quantity
quarantine
quarrel
questionnaire
quick
quiver
quizzical

r

rabble
rabies
raccoon
racial
racism
racket
racketeer
raconteur
racy
radial
radiant
radical
radioed
radish
radium
radius
raffia
raffle
raft
raged
ragged
raglan
ragout
raid
railing
raiment
rain
rainy
raisin
rakish
rally
ramble
ramification
rampage
rampant
rancid
random
range
rankle
ransom
rapacious
rarely
rarity
raspberry
ratchet
rateable
rather
ratio
ration
rationalize
rattle
rattlesnake
raucous
ravage
ravel
raven
raw
rayon
raze
razor
reach
reaction
reactor
reader
readily
ready
realism
reality
really
reap
reason
reasonable
rebait
rebate
rebel
rebellion
rebuke
rebuttal
recalcitrate
recapitulate
recede
receipt
recent
reception
recess
recession
recipe
reciprocal
reciprocity
recital
recitation
reckless
reckon
reclamation
recluse
recognize
recommend
recompense
reconnoitre
record
recoup
recovery
recreation
recriminatory
recruit
rectal
rectangle
rectify
recuperate
recurrence
redemption
redden
reduce
reducible
redundant
reentry
refer
reference
refinement
reflection
reflex
reform
reformation

refrain
refrigerator
refugee
refurbish
refusal
regal
regale
regardless
regency
regime
regiment
region
register
regression
regrettable
regular
regulate
regurgitate
rehabilitate
rehearsal
rehearse
Reich
reindeer
reinforce
reject
rejoice
rejuvenate
relation
relative
relax
release
relegate
relentless
relevant
reliable
reliant
relied
relief
relieve
religious
relinquish
relish
reluctance
rely
remain
remedial
remedy
remember
reminisce
remission
remit
remittance
remittent
remnant
remonstrate
remorseful
remote
removable
removal
remunerate
renaissance
rendezvous
renegade
renege
renew
renovate
reorganize
repair
reparable
repartee
repeal
repeat
repel
repellent
repercussion
repertory
repetition
replacement
replete
replica
reply
repository
reprehensible
represent
repressed
reprieve
reprimand
reprisal
reprise
reprobate
reproduce
reptile
republic
republican
repugn
reputable
require
requisite
requittal
resalable
rescind
research
resemblance
resent
reservation
reservoir
residence
residual
residue
resign
resilience
resin
resistance
resistible
resolution
resolve
resonance
resort
resource
respectable
respirator
respite
responsible
restoration
result
resume
resumption
resurrection
resuscitate
retail
retain
retaliate
reticent
retina
retire
retirement
retouch
retribution
retrieve
retrogression
retrospect
retroussé
reveal
reveille
revelation
revenge
revenue
reverent
reverie
reversible
revert
revise
revision
revival
revocation
revolt
revolution
rewrite
rhapsody
rheostat
rhetoric
rheumatism
rhinestone
rhinoceros
rhododendron
rhubarb
rhyme
rhythm
ribald
ribbon
rickety
rickshaw
riddance
riddle
ridge
ridiculous

rifle
right
righteous
rigid
rigmarole
rigour
rigorous
ringer
rinsing
riot
riotous
ripe
ripen
ripple
rise
rising
risqué
ritual
rival
rivet
roam
roaring
roast
robbery
robin
robot
rock
rocket
rococo
rogue
roguish
romance
roofs
rosary
rose
rosin
rotary
rotten
roué
rouge
rough
roulette
routine
roving
royal
royally
rubber
rudder
rude
ruler
rumba
rumble
rummage
rummy
rumour
runner
running
rupture
rural
russet
Russia
rustic
rustle
rye

S

Sabbath
sabotage
saccharin
sacrament
sacred
sacrilegious
safety
said
salad
salami
salary
salmon
salve
sandwich
sanitation
sapphire
sarcastic
sarsaparilla
satellite
satisfaction
satisfactory
Saturday
sauerkraut
sausage
saving
scarce
scarcely
scarcity
scare
scene
scenic
sceptical
schedule
scheme
schism
scholar
scholastic
schooner
science
scissors
Scripture
scythe
season
secede
secession
secretary
sedan
seduce
seeing
seem
segregate
seize
seizure
seldom
select
selfish
selves
semester
senator
senior
sensitive
separate
September
sergeant
series
sermon
service
serviceable
settee
seventh
several
sexy
sheath
sheik
shelves
shepherd
sherbet
sheriff
shield
shillelagh
shining
shipment
shipped
should
shoulders
shouldn't
shove
shriek
siege
sieve
signature
significant
silence
silhouette
similar
sincere
situation
sixth
skeleton
slaughter
socialist
society
sofa
soften
solar
solder
soldier
solemn
sophisticate
sophomore

sorrow
sorry
southern
souvenir
sovereign
Soviet Union
spaghetti
Spaniard
special
specify
specimen
speech
spirit
sponsor
stalk
starboard
statement
stating
statistic
status
staunch
stealthy
stomach
stopped
straitjacket
strength
strenuous
strenuously
stretch
strictly
struggle
study
studying
suave
submarine
subordinate
subpoena
subscription
subsistence
subtle
suburb
suburban
succeed
success

successor
succinct
suede
sufficient
suffix
suffrage
suggest
suggestion
summary
superfluous
supersede
supplies
supply
suppose
suppress
surface
surgeon
surgery
surmise
surplus
surprise
surround
surveillance
survey
survival
survive
suspicion
sword
syllable
symbol
symmetrical
symmetry
sympathy
symphony
symptom
syndicate
synthetic
syringe
syrup
system

t

tablet
taboo
tabulate
tacit
tackle
tact
tactics
taffeta
tailor
taint
Taiwan
taking
talent
tangent
tangible
tantalize
tantrum
target
tariff
tarnish
tasting
tattered
tattle
tattoo
tawdry
teach
tearful
technical
technique
tedious
teenager
telegram
telephone
television
temerity
temperament
temperance
temperature
template
temporarily
temporary
tempt
temptation
tenable
tenacious
tenacity

tenant
tendency
tendentious
tendon
tenement
tenet
Tennessee
tenor
tension
tentacle
tentative
tenuous
tepee
tepid
tequila
terminal
terminate
termite
terms
terrain
terrestrial
terrible
terribly
terrific
terrify
territorial
territory
terror
terse
testament
testify
testimony
tetanus
textbook
textile
texture
Thailand
theatre
theft
their
theirs
theme
themselves
theology

heorem
heory
herapeutic
hermonuclear
hermostat
hesaurus
hese
hesis
hief
hieves
hirsty
hirteen
horough
hough
housand
hread
hreat
hreshold
thrifty
thrilling
thriving
throat
thug
thwart
tiara
tickle
tier
tight
till
timid
timorous
timpani
tin
tingle
tinsel
tiny
tip-off
tirade
tithe
titillate
title
titular
toady
tobacco

toboggan
today
toga
together
toilet
token
tolerant
toll
tomato
tomb
tombstone
tomorrow
tongue
tonic
tonight
tonnage
tonsil
tonsillectomy
tooth
topic
Torah
toreador
torment
tornado
torpedo
torpor
torque
torrent
torrid
totalling
tour
tragedy
transfer
treachery
tremendous
treasurer
tried
tries
triplicate
triumph
trouble
truly
truthfully
tryst

Tuesday
tulip
tumult
turpentine
turpitude
twelfth
tying
type
typewriter
tyrant

u

ubiquitous
ukulele
ulcer
ulterior
ultimate
ultimatum
umbilical
umbrage
umbrella
umpire
unacceptable
unanimous
unavoidable
uncertain
uncle
uncommon
unconditional
unconscious
uncontrollable
uncouth
unctuous
undeniable
underground
underprivileged
understand
undertaker
underwrite
underwriter
undesirable
undoubtedly
undress
undue

unduly
undying
unearned
unearth
uneasy
unemployed
unequal
unequivocal
unerring
unfair
unfavourable
unfinished
unfit
unforgettable
unfortunate
unfriendly
ungodly
ungrateful
unhealthy
unholy
uniform
unify
unilateral
unique
unison
unit
Unitarian
united
unity
universally
universe
university
unkempt
unknowable
unmistakable
unnamed
unnatural
unnecessary
unoccupied
unpleasant
unpopular
unprejudiced
unprincipled
until

usable
used to
useful
using
usually

V

vaccination
vacillate
vacuum
valentine
valid
valour
valuable
valve
vandal
vanilla
vanish
vanity
vapid
vaquero
variable
variety
various
vase
vassal
Vatican
vaudeville
vector
vegetable
vehement
vehicle
veil
vein
velocity
venal
veneer
venerable
veneration
Venetian
vengeance
Venice
venom
venomous
ventilate
ventriloquist
veracity
verbal
verbally
verifiable
verification
verify
verily
verity
vermin
vermouth
vernacular
versatile
verse
versification
versify
versus
vertebra
vertebral
vertebrate
vertical
vessel
vested
vestibule
vestige
veteran
veterinary
vetoes
vex
viable
vibrant
vice
vicinity
vicious
victim
victory
Vietnam
vigil
vigilance
vigorous
vigour
vilify
village
villain
vindicate
vinegar
violet
violin
viper
virgin
virtue
virulence
virulent
visage
visible
vital
vitally
vitamin
vitiate
vivid
vocabulary
voice
volume
voluntary
vomit
vulgar

W

wafer
wagon
waken
wallet
walnut
wanton
warble
warden
warehouse
warning
warp
warranty
warrior
wary
wassail
wastage
waylaid
wealth
weapon
weather
wedding
Wednesday
weird
welcome
welfare
western
whereof
whether
while
whippersnapper
whippoorwill
whisk
whisky
whistle
white
who
wholesale
wholesome
wicked
wild
wilderness
wince
wintry
wisdom
wither
withhold
wives
wizard
wolves
womb
women
won
wondrous
world
worm
worship
worsted
wound
wrangle
wrath
wreath
wreck
wrestle

vretch
vriggle
vrinkle
vrist
vrithe
vriting
vritten
vrong

x

Xavier
Xmas
x-ray
xylophone

y

yacht
yearned
yellow
yeoman
yesterday
yield
yodel
yoga
yogurt (or: yoghurt)
yonder
you all
youngster
yours
yourself

z

zeal
zenith
zephyr
Zeus
zinc
zither
Zodiac
zoology